I0824421

REDEFINE RETIREMENT AND NEVER PEAK ON YOUR FINANCIAL JOURNEY

CREATING YOUR WORK-OPTIONAL LIFESTYLE

A PURPOSE-DRIVEN PLAN FOR FINANCIAL FREEDOM

JEREMY L. DAVIS

Creating Your Work-Optional Lifestyle: A Purpose-Driven Plan for Financial Freedom

Published by:
Aviva Publishing
Lake Placid, NY
(518) 523-1320
www.AvivaPubs.com

Address all inquiries to:
Jeremy L. Davis
1814 Ridgetrail Lane
Castle Rock, CO 802014
(303) 668-0077
jd@livingyourworkoptionallife.com
www.LivingYourWorkOptionalLife.com

ISBN: 978-1-63618-150-9
Library of Congress Control Number: 2021916974

Editors: Tyler Tichelaar and Larry Alexander, Superior Book Productions
Cover Design: Nicole Gabriel, Angel Dog Productions
Interior Book Layout: Nicole Gabriel, Angel Dog Production
Author Photo: Kim Benfield

Every attempt has been made to properly source all quotes.
Printed in the United States of America
First Edition
2 4 6 8 10 12

DEDICATION

This book is dedicated to Leo Porter, my grandfather.

He taught me about life, how to be a good man, and that nothing ventured is nothing gained.

ACKNOWLEDGMENTS

Thank you to Jenny Kronbach for setting the stage, loving me for who I am, and getting me off the blocks with this project.

Thank you to my sister, Christy, for believing in my dreams.

Thank you to my dad, Lee Davis, and mother, Kathryn Davis, for providing life to me and the best example of a life well lived.

Lastly, to my beloved children, Sloane and Eli. I love you more than anything in the whole wide world. You have taught me more than I will ever teach you.

CONTENTS

full
part
time

INTRODUCTION

On a blustery Wednesday afternoon high in the Colorado Rockies, I was working as a ski technician at the base of a major ski resort. I had graduated from college a couple of years earlier and was searching for a lifestyle that would be fun, plus I wanted to live in a place where everyone else was on vacation. I wanted to live the dream! Unfortunately, my dream became a nightmare. After about a year of having fun, I was broke, I had just been severely injured in a ski accident, and I was working an hourly job that had no upside. What I thought would be a fun, unique lifestyle had turned into a depressing, monotonous grind while I watched everyone else have the time of their life. Fortunately, that blustery Wednesday had brought my father in for a visit to have lunch with me. We hadn't seen each other for a while, so he said he wanted to come up to pay me a visit and see where I worked.

We had lunch at a beautiful wooden lodge on the ski resort with an incredible view of the snowcapped peaks all around. Dad and I exchanged the usual pleasantries over hamburgers and fries. I was still in an arm sling from a recent skiing accident, which had broken my humerus bone and nearly ended my life when I hit a tree at thirty-plus miles per hour. I was a bit depressed, to say the least. My father, sensing something was off, asked me how I was doing. My response was not so good. I told him I felt like I was at a dead-end hourly job; I was broke, broken, and depressed. I couldn't do the one thing I loved—skiing—because of my injury. I could barely pay my bills in an expensive resort town, and I told him I felt a bit lost. To add more drama, I had recently separated from a longtime girlfriend who had moved overseas. I let him know my situation had not ended up the way I had fantasized it would after graduating from college, and I felt I needed a change.

While I was complaining, a lightbulb went off in my head. It was midday on a Wednesday, yet he was up here in this beautiful place to listen to me. *Shouldn't he be at work?* I thought. *Was he skipping out on his responsibilities to hang out with me?* I stopped my diatribe right then and asked him a simple question. "How can you be up here on a random Wednesday in the middle of a workweek just to have lunch with me?" His response changed the trajectory of my life. He said, "I can do pretty much whatever I want these days. I've saved enough money to have the choice to work, come see you, or go hang out with anyone. My business produces income whether or not I'm in the office, and my investments and savings produce income that can last for a lifetime, so all my bills are paid no matter what I'm doing on a given day. I'm here because I want to be here with my son." At that moment, I stopped him and asked, "So, does that mean you are retired?" He paused for a moment and said, "Retirement is not for me; it's a concept that will never be for me. I love what I'm doing, and I intend to keep doing it for my entire life." He expanded on this, telling me that he felt useful and wanted to be engaged with his work as long as he was blessed with good health and the knowledge to genuinely help his clients. He also mentioned a few examples of people he knew who had worked and saved their entire lives while engaged in careers they didn't like just to retire and die a few years later. Retirement to him was quitting on the opportunity life offered, which for him was to provide his unique value to society.

As an early twenty-something, my mind was blown. Why would my father still want to work if he had all the resources not to? His response was simple. He wanted to design his life around putting energy into activities he was really passionate about. He said he was really lucky to operate a business that helped people with their money, and he never wanted to stop. He just wanted to make sure he had the financial options to spend his time in ways he felt were most productive to his life's purpose. At the time of that conversation, my dad was in his mid-forties. Fast forward to today and my dad is sixty-five, enjoying his life, and continuing to work when and how he *wants* to, with the resources to spend his time in any way he sees fit, and he coaches his clients to do the same. His example and several others have convinced me that my previous concept of "retirement" was flawed.

After that day, I decided to embark on a journey not only to understand retirement, but to understand money, how it works, and what it can do to serve people on their life's journey. I quit my job in the ski industry to become a certified financial planner. In the early years of my career, I interviewed hundreds of potential clients about their goals and beliefs. During the process, I built a successful business coaching people on how to succeed with their money. I found that very few people actually knew what they wanted out of retirement. Many of them gazed at the ceiling when I asked them how much money they would need on a monthly basis to retire. For most, it was a very vague and ambiguous process that hardly ever resulted in a concrete figure or a defined age unless I gave them some general guidelines that were given to me by the financial industry's textbooks. If we succeeded at identifying an amount and an age, very few of them actually stuck to that target and continued to work in one form or another, even after they were financially prepared. Not only that, but they expressed very little excitement around the topic. Some viewed it as a way not to work anymore, but they had no idea what they would do with their time. Others viewed retirement as scary and too far away to have any idea what it meant. I knew I had to develop a process that made it easy for people to consider their financial independence and to design a plan to get them there.

Over the last twenty years as a professional wealth advisor, I have crafted a plan and a process to reshape the concept of retirement. I've accomplished this through the school of hard knocks, feedback from thousands of individual clients and friends, and countless hours of research. My financial planning practice now manages more than half-a-billion dollars of assets and has helped hundreds of people achieve their version of a work-optional lifestyle because I have asked the right questions and helped them apply the process outlined in the following pages. By applying this process to my own personal situation, I have found fulfillment, wealth, and purpose. I've been encouraged by family, friends, and clients to share this process with more people, and this book is my way of doing just that.

I hope you will read this book to find out how to make your life work-optional yet purposeful. Welcome to a work-optional lifestyle plan, no matter where you are on your financial journey.

Enjoy!

full
part
time

CHAPTER 1

COMING ALIVE

"Though no one can go back and make a brand-new start, anyone can start from now and make a brand-new ending."

— Carl Bard

MONEY ISN'T EVERYTHING

What if you decided not to go into work tomorrow? What would happen? I'm sure you could probably call in sick, or take a personal day. Most likely people wouldn't begin to ask questions, and you would easily be able to escape work for one day. What if you decided to take the next two weeks off? You might have some unused vacation or sick time to get you through. For some people, however, things might begin to break down here. After a few weeks of not going to work, perhaps you wouldn't get paid and your bills would begin to pile up. Obligations would not be met, and your coworkers might begin to wonder where you are and if you'll ever return.

What if you decided to take the next month off? Would your bills get paid? Would things keep running smoothly at home and at work? Odds are you picked up this book because you are one of the many people who can't just stop going to work without serious consequences. During a month off, you might struggle to keep the mortgage paid, keep the lights on, and keep a healthy balance in your savings account—if you had one to begin with. If you were to stretch that time out even farther, you might have to dig into your retirement plan money, or even worse, borrow on the equity in your house.

If your resources would be stretched to the breaking point if you didn't go to work to earn an income, then the strategies presented in the following pages represent more freedom and possibility than you can imagine. This purpose-driven plan for a work-optional lifestyle is an antidote to personal financial chaos.

Motivational speaker Zig Ziglar once said, "Money isn't everything, but it's right up there next to oxygen." If you knew there was enough money coming in regardless of whether you went to work, my guess is you'd have plenty of oxygen! A work-optional lifestyle gives you the flexibility to work on your interests and to apply your effort to endeavors that give life meaning. A work-optional lifestyle isn't a license to sit on the beach and drink Mai-Tais while watching the waves crash. A work-optional lifestyle is about doing the work now to set up your life and finances around your purpose in life.

READ THE INSTRUCTIONS CAREFULLY

Growing up, I would always help my parents assemble items they purchased for our home. At the time, we didn't have much money, so it was less expensive to buy unstained furniture and "ready to assemble" household décor. Inevitably, there would be pieces left over at the end of each project.

Has this situation ever happened to you? Maybe when assembling the latest IKEA dresser? I would read the first few diagrams and follow along closely. When I thought I had it figured out, I would ignore the rest of the instructions. I thought the instructions were just there for people not smart enough to figure it out on their own. Quite often, I installed pieces incorrectly, ended up with extra parts, or ruined the item altogether. As I grew older, I accumulated more frustrating experiences like putting chair legs on backwards, having cold water come out of the faucet's hot tap, and best of all, installing a transmission wrong two times in my 1987 Blazer. I realized I would have saved an unbelievable amount of time, money, and frustration had I just gone from step one to step ten in the instruction manual.

This book is an instruction manual to help you achieve your work-optional lifestyle on your terms. If you read these instructions carefully, you may just surprise yourself. What I'm laying out in the following chapters is what I've learned over a twenty-year financial planning career by helping families through more than 8,000 client reviews, financial analyses, and personal financial plans. I've helped many of these individuals achieve their goal of living a work-optional lifestyle. And I want to help you!

Maybe your goal is to restore a classic car, fix up an old house, or write a book. If you knew your bills were taken care of, wouldn't you have the time to work on the things you want to work on instead of the things you have to work on? This book provides a roadmap and manual so you can do exactly that. I have created and refined this process and recorded it within these pages to help you get where you want to go. Are you ready?

THE CAVALRY ISN'T COMING

If you've watched the movie *The Pursuit of Happyness* featuring Will Smith, you know it's a story about Chris Gardner, a man who struggled through a divorce, homelessness, and poverty to become a successful stockbroker and wealth manager. Chris Gardner wrote the book *Start Where You Are* shortly after the motion picture was released. The book is his story about the lessons he learned along the way to becoming successful and overcoming adversity. In the book, he said, "The cavalry isn't coming; you have to start where you are." This is essential information because he understood nobody was going to save him. He knew he had to push through and make the right decisions, drag himself out of poverty, and become whom he was meant to be. The same holds true for anyone else looking to make their life better.

Most of us can't rely on inheritance, the lottery, or any other financial windfall. We must make our own way. The world is an unforgiving place, and nobody owes us anything. We have to do the right thing with our money and our attitude each and every day. We must do the hard work of staying disciplined to achieve our goals. Imaginary windfalls will not secure our future or improve our life. Putting off debts and paying minimums won't work. In short, the cavalry isn't coming, and it's up to us to become the master of our financial domain.

COMPOUND INTEREST

Einstein said, "Compound interest is the eighth wonder of the world. Those who understand it, earn it; those who don't, pay it." I happen to think he was dead right. To add to Einstein's comments, I would say compound cash flow is the ninth wonder of the world. Compound interest takes an extremely long amount of time to accumulate. If living a work-optional lifestyle is something you'd like to achieve, you will not have enough time for compound interest to work its magic. Instead, we're looking for compound cash flow. I'll expand on this concept in the following chapters, but it's vital to know that if your work-optional lifestyle is going to happen, you need to focus exclusively on compound cash flow.

If you take nothing else away from this book, take this concept and apply it across your financial life. You will be better for it! Compound cash flow is generated by positioning your money and time to generate recurring payments to yourself that you can rely on each month. If you add more time and money to this process, the payments continue to grow on each other, creating a cash flow snowball that cannot be stopped. Of course, there's a lot to do before we start installing a compound cash flow plan for you, but it deserves an explanation early on.

LEAVE THINGS BETTER THAN YOU FOUND THEM

So, we've established that: 1) Nobody's going to save you, 2) Compound cash flow is the key to living a work-optional life, and 3) Money is right up there in the hierarchy of human needs next to oxygen.

We are told that we stand on the shoulders of those who came before us. If you look back in your family tree, you can probably attribute some of your qualities to people who came before you. You can also attribute some of your not-so-good qualities to people who came before you. My challenge to you is to look at your life, look at your finances, and then change the path of your family forever. Leave your situation better than you found it. Leave more money to your family than anyone has before. Teach your children how money works; teach them to fix things up and sell them for a profit. Show your children you have made the right decisions in life. Use money as a tool to spend more time with your family. Show your family it's possible to gain true financial freedom!

CHALLENGE 1

Write down five things that are really important for you to do in your life. I challenge you to write down something meaningful! What would you work on? Whom would you hang out with? What hobbies would you get better at? What business would you like to build? There will be some tough stuff ahead and some truths to face, so be intentional about what you write here:

1.

2.

3.

4.

5.

full
part
time

Chapter 2

THE POWER OF NOW

"You may never know what results come from your actions. But if you do nothing, there will be no result."

— Mohandas Karamchand Gandhi

NOTHING VENTURED, NOTHING GAINED

Now that I've described a few of the key tenets of a work-optional life, it's time to get down to work. It's time to use the power of now to get your mind right and to act. The law of diminishing intent is real, which is why I've put challenges after each chapter throughout this book. The law of diminishing intent says your action threshold goes down as time moves forward. My plea is that you act now because you can gain tremendous traction in a short time. You can gain traction just like Rocky Balboa.

Sylvester Stallone was a nobody, a starving actor in New York. He was doing side jobs and trying out for part after part to no avail. Deciding that New York wasn't the promised land, Stallone moved to California to try his luck again. After a few failed auditions, he realized he was going to have to take desperate measures. He was forced to sell his dog for food and hock his ex-wife's jewelry to survive. That moment became the rock bottom turning point for Stallone, so he decided it was time to give it all he had. Inspired by a boxing match he saw on TV, Stallone stayed up twenty-one straight hours to write a screenplay about an underdog boxer who, against all odds, would beat the reigning world champion in the ring. Stallone knew if he didn't act then, he might end up broke and forgotten. He wrote that script, pouring his heart and soul into it.

A short while later, Stallone presented his script to some producers who had just rejected him for a part. Astonishingly, they liked his screenplay and offered him $25,000 to buy the rights. This was life-changing money for Stallone at the time. But Sly had bigger ideas. He rejected the offer, saying he wanted more money and the lead role as well. They negotiated back and forth until the offer reached $360,000 for the rights to the film, but without giving him the lead role. But Stallone was adamant—he wanted the lead role and rejected the offer again. Finally, the producers caved, offered him a budget of $1,000,000 to make the movie, and agreed he would retain the rights and play the lead.

Stallone bet on himself, and the rest is cinematic history. The screenplay he wrote in twenty-one hours was for *Rocky*. The 1976 film went on to become the first in one of the most successful franchises in movie history, grossing more than $1.4 billion. It won three Academy Awards, including Best Picture. The movie was produced on home video cameras and came in under its budget of $1 million, which is almost nothing in the movie business.

Stallone had hit rock bottom when he was inspired by a boxing match he saw on TV. He was desperate enough to "act now." He poured his heart and soul into a last-ditch effort to become successful. In just twenty-one hours, he changed the course of his life, and the lives of many generations of Stallones to come. His low-budget, piecemeal movie became a Hollywood sensation all because a desperate guy spent twenty-one hours of concentrated effort on attaining his dream.

When it comes to our money, we have a "someday" attitude about what we might do to improve our circumstances. Stallone had a "right now" attitude and sat down to write. This is the kind of action-taking mentality you need to harness to become successful with your money. Decide that work-optional is important enough to you for you to work really hard right now. My question to you is: Can you find twenty-one hours to change the course of your life? Could you find ten hours and become half as successful as Sylvester Stallone?

In the same spirit as Sylvester Stallone, my grandfather repeated this beautiful saying: "Nothing ventured, nothing gained." I think I've heard it elsewhere, but my grandfather was right next to God in my eyes. He had fought in the Korean War, raised seven children, and ran a successful business. Nothing seemed to faze him, and he always had this quiet confidence about him that I admired. He would use that saying when talking about how he had smuggled his pearl-handled revolver back from the Korean War, or when he fought a legal battle with one of the largest defense companies in North America for dumping toxic waste on his land. He was successful at everything he did, largely because he took action and had the courage to move forward, knowing if he gave it his best, things would generally work out.

My grandfather always took immediate action on challenges he felt strongly about, especially if they involved moral wrongdoing. He set out to have a big family, to be successful in business, and to live on an unshakable moral and religious foundation. My grandfather did absolutely everything it took to raise his family the right way. He would raise animals in the backyard to sell, and he would work around the clock to make sure there was food on the table. My mom once told me that he never, ever stopped working. Even late in his life, he went to work for fun. He knew that if he ventured out, took the chance, and put forth maximum effort, the results he was after would be there at the end of the day.

It's important to act, even if you don't know exactly what you're doing. Stallone and my grandfather just did it. One had had enough of being poor; the other just took action all the time. As you think about your ability to get your financial life organized, just act now. There is no time like the present!

THERE IS NO PLAN B

When John Elway hired Peyton Manning as the quarterback for my favorite football team, the Denver Broncos, in 2012, after Manning had enjoyed a thirteen-year career with the Indianapolis Colts, many questioned Manning's health. He had had four neck surgeries and people questioned if he could even throw the ball effectively anymore. When a reporter asked Elway in an interview just after Manning was hired, "What's your plan B if Peyton doesn't work out?" Elway chuckled and replied, "There is no plan B; we're going with plan A."

In his four years with Denver, Manning brought the Broncos to two Super Bowls, and they won one of them. It seems both Manning and Elway were committed to winning, no matter what.

When it comes to your finances and things that are really meaningful, you shouldn't have a plan B. My hope for you, dear reader, is that plan A is *your* plan for financial success, and it includes spending more time with your family and developing a quiet confidence that you are building a legacy for generations to come. Once you've read this book, plan A will be officially in motion. If you don't have a plan A, then *now* is the time to get one.

START WITH PLAN A

"What exactly should plan A do?" you ask. The saying is probably overused but..."If you don't have a plan, you're planning to fail." Your goal, at the end of these chapters, is to have the framework for putting a plan in place and starting down the path of righteousness, financial wellbeing, and peace. As I say to many of my clients, the pilot doesn't just get in the airplane and fly around, hoping to end up where they are supposed to be. There's always a definitive flight plan. The pilot will have to make course corrections along the way, but will have a plan, and ultimately, the plane lands where it's supposed to.

Along the way in your financial life, you will face ups and downs and emotional challenges. There will be financial ups and downs, there will be family ups and downs, and you will have to constantly adjust your own flight path to compensate for the turbulence. Your plan A is to take the challenges, answer the bell, and follow this guide.

CHALLENGE 2

Write down five things that will happen if you don't act now to achieve your work optional lifestyle. Examples might be "I'll be in debt forever," "I'll miss my chance to create a legacy for my family," or "I'll work forever in a job I hate."

1.

2.

3.

4.

5.

If you don't act now, you'll be another day/year/decade older than you are today. You may miss an opportunity in the market, you may die, you may be physically unable to do what you want to do. A million things could happen to derail your future. Just act now!

full
part
time

Chapter 3

MEANING AND MONEY

"And in the end, it's not the years in your life that count. It's the life in your years."

— Abraham Lincoln

CHILDREN HAVE IMPORTANT THINGS TO SAY

I have a ritual with my ten-year-old daughter, Sloane, every night before she goes to bed. We call it "question time." I do it for a few reasons, but the best reason is it's a time when it's just me and her and the rest of the world is silent. I want to encourage her to ask questions and to give her a forum where there are no distractions. One night as we were having our little daddy-daughter question time, Sloane asked me why I work so hard and what I did for people while I was away at work during the day. I didn't know it at the time, but my response to that question was another catalyst for writing this book. What I said to her was that I have some goals I'm trying to achieve so our life as a family could be better. I said I wanted to have more choices about how I spent my time each day. I fumbled around for a bit, and then I muttered, "I'm trying to make sure there's enough money coming in so I can spend more time doing the things I love."

Sloane's response was amazing. She said, "Daddy, if you can do that, doesn't it mean you can spend more time with me and Eli?" I said, "That's exactly right, sweetheart." If that's not moving, I don't know what is.

My resolve to be financially successful prior to that conversation was very strong, but Sloane's response that night definitely cemented it. I wanted to create lasting income streams that would allow me to spend more time with my daughter and son and also with other people I care about, to work on other projects I care about, and to put time into other causes I care about. Sloane's response that night further enhanced my mission.

I realize not everyone reading this book has children. Having children is not the point. The point is I care about my kids more than anything else on this planet. I attach my financial outcome to them, which is extraordinarily motivating and meaningful every day I'm fortunate enough to be living.

Perhaps you had doubters in your life. Maybe you'd like to impress upon your mother or father that you've become a success and can spend your time any way you see fit. Maybe the motivation comes from driving an old beat-up car every day, and you've just had enough of that piece of crap. Perhaps you're tired of looking at credit card or medical bills that you can't pay. The motivation to move down a different path can come from almost anywhere.

Another key motivational moment happened when I was a freshman in high school. I had a lot of energy as a young man and was very unfocused. I was also a late bloomer, so I was smaller than most of the boys my age. Because of these facts, I had a propensity to attract attention by being somewhat of a class clown.

My ninth-grade geometry teacher, Mr. Robinson, didn't take kindly to my antics. He didn't like me, and I did not like him. One day, I was sitting in his class desperately trying to focus on the concept he was teaching—probably about a rhombus or an obtuse angle or something. For once, I wasn't talking or causing any sort of disturbance. He looked at me, singled me out in front the whole class, and said, "Look at you, Davis. You're just riding your desk, just going through the motions like always."

I had my hands on the front of the desk, trying to focus on what he was saying. However, I was singled out as a slacker and a do-nothing. He was making fun of me as the rest of the class roared with laughter. I was the joke. Teachers aren't supposed to behave that way, but Mr. Robinson became a great motivator for me for the rest of my life. I was determined from then on to no longer go through the motions. I was getting terrible grades at the time and thought nothing of it, until that moment.

Going forward, I decided to put some honest effort into my studies and attempt to get into a decent college. I slowly rebuilt my failing grades, turning them into passing marks over the subsequent years. Ultimately, I was accepted at a division one state university after a lot of lost time getting terrible grades and being totally immature.

The story gets better. After my freshman year of college, I was making ends meet financially by working on the grounds crew at a local golf course. One morning, my boss sent me out to dig a drainage ditch on the fairway to move water that had collected from some heavy rains. As I was digging the ditch, none other than Mr. Robinson pulled up on his golf cart. He looked at me and shook his head with a cocky grin. I could just sense what he must've been saying to himself. Probably something like, "I knew the kid wouldn't amount to anything. He was just going through the motions and still is." Not that digging a ditch isn't noble; it is—all work is. But the judgment I felt from him really made a difference to the rest of my life.

I don't know what Mr. Robinson is doing today. I do know that those two moments in my life were big inflection points. I was motivated by Mr. Robinson thinking I wouldn't amount to anything. I often think about that day on the golf course and what it meant to me. Sometimes, someone believing you can't do something is enough to get you over the top. Since that day, almost twenty years ago, I have become a multimillionaire, and I run successful real estate and finance businesses. I use this story as an example to help you find motivation deep within and start on a different path.

Where is your motivation? Is it a chip on your shoulder? Is it helping a family member? Do you have a higher purpose that gets you out of bed in the morning? Before you can move to the nuts and bolts of financial freedom, you need meaningful motivation attached to your financial outcome.

FINDING JOY

Perhaps there's no chip on your shoulder, no underlying reason to get out of bed in the morning, and maybe you don't have family members to take care of. Perhaps your motivation comes from having more moments of joy. Happiness is a destination rarely reached, but joy is all around us if we look for it. Financial freedom and living a work-optional lifestyle will provide you with the freedom to seek more moments of joy.

People say that kids grow up fast. They say you must work hard and grind away so one day you can retire and start to enjoy all the things you missed during your working life. Perhaps you'd like to take in a few more sunsets or sunrises. Maybe you just want to take a walk in the morning and enjoy being outside. Watching the birds fly about and listening to them sing on a beautiful spring day at the park could be just what you need to maintain focus and clarity. I know I love to watch my children play, to take them to the park, and to take them on walks through our neighborhood.

Take a second to think about what gives you complete joy. Would it be powerful to have the financial resources to enjoy more of those moments? Do moments of joy give you meaning?

MONEY KARMA: DOING THE RIGHT THINGS CREATES MORE RIGHT THINGS

Okay, so I've spent some time on motivations to attach your money habits to. Whether it's a high school teacher planting a chip firmly on your shoulder, finding moments of joy, or your kids motivating you to be a better steward of your money so you can spend more time with them, if you have found your motivation, you have a visceral reason to begin putting the pieces together for your work-optional life.

The last subject I'll talk about in the motivation area is karma. Karma is a Sanskrit word used in Buddhism and Hinduism. It means "the sum of a person's actions in this and previous states of existence viewed as deciding their fate in future existences." The informal definition of the word karma is "Fate following as the effect from a cause." Karma, in its most basic sense as a concept, means good intent and good deeds contribute to future good deeds and happiness. Therefore, the opposite of karma would be bad deeds and bad intent, leading to future misdeeds and suffering.

Many Americans have bad money karma, as evidenced by nearly 40 million households having no retirement savings at all, according to the National Institute on Retirement Security. In addition, the Employee Benefit Research Institute estimates Americans collectively have a retirement savings deficit of $4.3 trillion. To make matters even more exciting, according to the US Census Bureau, the average American between ages thirty-five and forty has a net worth, excluding home-equity, of $14,226.00. These statistics illustrate that most Americans have bad money karma. This means they make bad financial decisions, which compound over time, leading to a state of financial suffering.

What I've noticed in interviews with financial planning clients is that the ones who execute good money habits and have attached meaning and motivation to their money receive good money karma. For example, a good friend and client of mine had just paid his mortgage off at age thirty-seven. He did that because he has a plan to live a work-optional lifestyle at age fifty. When he told me he was done paying his mortgage, I was so excited for him. What was even more exciting was I got a call two weeks later from him to tell me he had received the biggest bonus of his career, and he wanted to know where to put the money since he had no more financial obligations. We have been working together on his work-optional lifestyle plan and invested the money so it would earn tax-free income down the road. My friend has had great money karma, and regular financial windfalls have been bestowed upon him and his wife because they are so disciplined with their money. Good financial behavior creates a compounding karmic effect. I've seen good money karma get results over and over again in my career.

CHALLENGE 3

Write down up to five life events that have motivated you, or put a chip on your shoulder to do better. For example, I had a teacher, Mr. Robinson, who told me I wouldn't amount to anything. This left a chip on my shoulder to show him I could become successful, so I would write "Mr. Robinson" in the first position on the list below. Maybe you drive a beat-up car that motivates you to be better, or perhaps a family member put you down or someone didn't believe in you along the way. Write their names down, or put the make and model of your beat-up car in the list to motivate you. Use this list as motivation any time you get off track on your plan to remind yourself why you want to be financially successful.

1.

2.

3.

4.

5.

Now let's take a moment to pause on the last few challenges. In the first challenge, you identified the important things you will do with your time once you achieve a work-optional lifestyle. In the second challenge, you identified what will happen if you don't act now. With Challenge 3, you have a reason pushing you forward to become more financially successful. It's important to have a why behind your money goals, and these challenges are meant to bring that out.

full
part
time

Chapter 4

FOLLOWING THE HERD

"Let our advance worrying become advance thinking and planning."

— Winston Churchill

TRADITIONAL ADVICE IS FLAWED

Now that you have found your deeply personal reasons to get your financial house in order and you have begun the journey to living a work-optional lifestyle, I must ask you to clear your mind and be open to the fact that your current financial plan may not be serving you all that well. If you have debt outside of your home mortgage, if you don't understand how much money you make each month, or if you don't have enough savings to last for six months to a year, you've been sold the wrong financial plan. If you don't have income from someplace other than your job, you've also been sold the wrong financial plan.

Traditional advice in America says to save 10 percent of your income toward retirement and put three months of expenses aside for emergencies. Also, try to save for your children's college educations and hope that you have enough insurance to take care of your family if something catastrophic happens. This financial advice doesn't seem to be working, given that half the country is broke, and most people couldn't afford one month of emergencies, let alone three. We've been believing the market will always go up over time and saving a measly 10 percent of our income will land us in this magical place where at age sixty-five we'll have the ability to live out our dreams on a fixed income as our body begins to succumb to biological reality. That plan has many flaws and doesn't address reality in most American households. Yes, it will get you to a better place financially than if you do nothing. It's a serviceable mantra for those who want to ignore reality and not do the deep work it takes to model your future and take charge of your money.

The work-optional life plan you are about to embark on does away with traditional advice, and redirects your focus on the here and now—on what you can do today to find your small piece of freedom and have the financial wherewithal to satisfy your curiosities. The human brain cannot conceptualize thirty to forty years of savings or what a person's life and money will look like then. The human brain can barely map out the next three to five years. The key to your work-optional life plan is starting small, being focused, and working forward from there. So, in this chapter, we're going to do away with traditional financial advice and prove why a work-optional life plan is a better choice.

THE OLD 401(K) IS DEAD

Okay, so I was a little hard on the old 401(k) in the subtitle above, but it got your attention. A 401(k) is a decent savings tool designed to provide you with income later in life and to give you tax benefits on money you save in the plan. Here's what's interesting to me about the traditional 401(k) plan; let's say you save $100,000 in your plan, you wait twenty-five years for the money to "grow," and you end up with $1 million. This is a very simple example, but if you're investing in a traditional 401(k), that $100,000 investment potentially saved you $25,000 in taxes. Now let's look at what the Federal Government gets on the compound growth of that $100,000.

The market hopefully grew your investment to $1 million, and now you're able to take it out over your retirement. Doing the simple math, it would appear to me the Federal Government does a lot better on your $1 million than you did on your original $100,000 investment. Let's say you took out $50,000 per year and paid $15,000 in federal income tax each year. Assuming those $50,000 withdrawals lasted for twenty years, the Federal Government just made $300,000 in future tax revenue. This is a brilliant way for the government to secure your future, isn't it? They miss out on $25,000 in tax over the short term and gain $300,000 in tax over the long term.

Many workers in America have a Roth 401(k) option in their company-sponsored plan. With this style of plan, you pay the tax on the money you put in, and it never gets taxed again (for the time being). This is a better option in the long run, especially if you are under age fifty-five.

I'm not illustrating these points to say whether or not a 401(k) is a good means of saving for a work-optional lifestyle. In many cases, it is a decent savings vehicle and a good means of automatic saving for the future (the very distant future). My point is the traditional advice you receive and the structure the Federal Government has provided is self-interested. I don't know if you've paid attention to Social Security recently, but that plan is on unstable footing, to say the least, and it's provided to you by none other than your Federal Government. The presupposition that the government can design plans that work well for the individual is flawed. Putting your money away in a 401(k) just so you can compound tax revenue for the Federal Government is not my idea of financial freedom.

The sage advice of "save in your 401(k)" should be carefully scrutinized. Hence, it is the first key financial topic we're going to dispense with. Your 401(k) should be looked at, after you've implemented your work-optional strategy as laid out in the chapters ahead, as a way to pay late life healthcare expenses, save on taxes now or in the future, and capture some employer money. It should not be the first-choice panacea the financial media proclaims it to be. We've got a lot of ground to cover before you start blindly saving into a 401(k) plan.

YOUR HOME IS A LIABILITY

Robert Kiyosaki's book *Rich Dad Poor Dad* put forth the concept that your home is a liability, not an asset. Kiyosaki has faced criticism for this thought-provoking idea. In my opinion, his belief is true if you carry a mortgage and have nothing but your work income to pay it each month.

To make a blanket statement like that takes some tremendous guts. As with the 401(k), the most common advice out there is to buy a home as soon as you can. Well, that makes sense on the surface, and it's getting your piece of the American Dream, but we need to understand that when you buy a home, you've also bought a stream of payments. If you've bought a stream of payments and have to work to make those payments, then I would have to agree with Kiyosaki—your home is a liability, not an asset.

That being said, everyone needs a place to live, and the average American spends between 15 and 42 percent of their income on housing, depending on where they live. Also, according to a 2016 "How Housing Matters Survey," commissioned by the Chicago-based nonprofit, John D. and Catherine T. MacArthur Foundation, and carried out by Hart Research Associates, more than 53 percent of Americans had to make at least one major financial sacrifice to pay their rent or mortgage in 2016. If that doesn't scream *liability* to you, then we come from different planets.

The key to purchasing a home is to design a plan to ensure mortgage payments are as small of a percentage of your income as possible. Then figure out what it would take either to pay it off quickly or develop enough income through your work-optional life plan to make the payment for you.

Let's say your take-home pay is $4,000 per month. Your take-home pay is defined as the amount you receive after taxes and other withholdings. In this case, you should spend no more than $1,000 to $1,400 a month on your mortgage, taxes, and insurance. Your work-optional life plan may be just to live without a mortgage. If that's the case, you want to develop enough savings or income-producing investments to passively pay $1,000 to $1,400 per month on your mortgage. Alternatively, you could live on nothing and pay down the mortgage as fast as possible. Once either of the two options above are accomplished, your home becomes an asset because it's no longer taking effort and time to make the payments. You could then sell it and bank a significant amount of cash.

In summary, the concept that your house is an asset is flawed only to the extent that you have to exert effort to make the payments. If the mortgage is being paid off through passive income and or extreme budgeting, then, and only then, does your home become an asset because it retains value and does not take cash flow away from you.

RULES TO LIVE BY

Following common rules of finance, and watching Public Television to get your financial advice, can get you messed up in all sorts of ways. The sage advice of "invest in your 401(k) and save three to six months' of savings in a savings account for a rainy day" are fundamentally flawed and backward, as I illustrated earlier. I call this plan the "Grow Old and Hope Plan." It's easy for others to tell you what to do without giving guidance on why and without any understanding of your specific situation.

Most people who have come to me for basic financial advice have had it all backward. They say, "I started saving in my 401(k), and I've got a couple of months' of emergency savings. Don't you think I'm doing great?" When I dive deeper, I discover they have student loans, car loans, and in many cases, they are paying way too much for housing. I certainly think it's great that they're saving, but they're paying more interest than they're earning each month in their 401(k) and emergency savings plan. Then the client says, "Well, my parents, friends, or Suze Orman told me to save in my 401(k) and put together an emergency savings plan." Isn't that what I'm supposed to be doing? Of course, my answer is most certainly *no*.

My advice is to look more closely to see what is siphoning money away from you each month. This is the first step to complete financial understanding. Looking through your expenses each month, you can find things that are siphoning money from you. If you can figure out how to limit the number of things siphoning money away from you, like car payments, credit card payments, student loans, mortgages, and insurance premiums, that is the first step to a financial awakening. The term I like to use for this process is, "Finding your cash flow resistance." In other words, what is sucking your income away that is not completely necessary?

In the scenario above, I advised this client to stop everything and start focusing on understanding their personal cash flow resistance. Understanding your personal cash flow is the first and most critical place along your journey. It is as simple as itemizing your inflows (your after-tax income) and your outflows (your expenses) over one month. You have to apply "chip on your shoulder" intensity and put in the work it takes to understand your personal expenses and income. If you can do this process for just three months, you will have something special: a foundation for understanding your personal cash flow. This exercise will help you understand the unbelievably large percentage of income you spend each month that creates no additional value.

Once I show people how much they are spending on restaurants, entertainment, automobile payments, cable TV, and cell phone bills, they almost become sick to their stomachs. It's incredible for them to see the percentage of their income they are spending on frivolous items. Once we have that figure in hand, we can begin taking serious action. This is the first step to financial freedom. Once you nail this exercise and actually quantify where your money is going each month, you begin to understand that, at a minimum, you could potentially start saving up to 20 percent of your take-home income. You have to eliminate the unwanted expenses that are causing your cash flow resistance each month.

The lesson here is to be very suspicious of the common wisdom pedaled by mainstream financial gurus. If you have credit card debt, student loans, or car payments, the first step in your work-optional lifestyle plan is to stop everything and measure your cash flow resistance. Once you measure your cash flow resistance, you can begin the process of moving into cash flow freedom!

CHALLENGE 4

List five monthly expenses siphoning money from you that in no way are improving your quality of life. In other words, I want you to measure your cash flow resistance. Do you carry a balance on a credit card? Do you have a student loan that's been around for ten or fifteen years? Do you eat out all the time? Honestly consider whether each of the expenses below is worth you not reaching your goals.

1.

2.

3.

4.

5.

Now, add up the dollar amount of those expenses. What percentage of your income is it? Simply divide the dollar amount by your take-home pay. It's time to eliminate the cash flow resistance and start cancelling these expenses. Take the saved money and invest it each month into your work-optional plan. You will want to use the strategies in the following chapters for this money.

full
part
time

Chapter 5

NOTHING BUT THE BASICS

"The man who moves a mountain begins by carrying away small stones."

— Confucius

INCOME IS THE OUTCOME

Your income, and your ability to grow it, is the single most important factor in determining your financial success. That factor is not how the stock market does, not interest rates, and most certainly not who is president. It's about you and your income.

If you measured your cash flow resistance in the previous chapter, then you've gleaned the first understanding into the power of your income. Let's say you found 10 percent of your income that you were able to liberate from cash flow resistance. Then you decided to put that money to work. You put it away each month into an income-producing investment with the goal to have the income from that investment eventually make your mortgage payment for you. Wouldn't that exercise be extremely helpful? You've taken a resource that you already have and started leveraging it for your future benefit. It's incredible how fast the dollars add up once you eliminate cash flow resistance and get rid of unnecessary expenses.

Perhaps your goal isn't to have your mortgage paid. Maybe you're thinking about taking a trip every year and you want one of your investments to pay for that. Maybe you want a vacation home, but you don't want to deal with all the expenses that come with it. Maybe you want to have a little income each month so you don't have to work as much. If you have enough income without having to work for it, the sky is the limit. The only thing holding you back then is you!

One of my personal goals was to save enough money so I could have a vacation home in the mountains and not have to rely on my work income or effort to pay for it. I set out to have enough passive cash flow coming in to pay my mortgage and expenses on this mountain home by the time I was thirty-five. I knew the mortgage and expenses would cost me around $1,000 per month. I worked the numbers backwards to figure out the lump sum I would need to save to produce $1,000 per month of cash flow. By my estimates, I needed $120,000 to produce that income every month using a high-income, high-risk investment vehicle.

That $120,000 was a lot of money to me at age thirty-two when I originally set the goal. At the time, I had a golf club membership and a fancy sports car, and they both had payments that were siphoning away a significant portion of my monthly income. I would come home from the golf course mad because I didn't play well. I didn't use the sports car at all other than for the occasional night out on the town. I took a hard look at my financial life and decided what I was doing with my money wasn't me. I had a fancy car to impress people I didn't like, and I was playing a sport I wasn't good at that made me feel like a total loser. I felt I was living somebody else's life to somehow fulfill a version of someone I thought somebody else might be impressed by. I needed to be me. I wanted to have a mountain home, and I had all this other *stuff* taking my money away from the things and lifestyle I truly desired.

I was able to sell the stupid car, quit the golf club, and apply that money toward my goal of having a mountain home. Over the next four years, my income went up. I also focused on eliminating unnecessary expenses that didn't improve my life and didn't define who I was, and I started applying money to my real goals. It took me a little longer than I thought, but by age thirty-seven, my wife and I had purchased the home, and its mortgage and expenses are now all paid for each month by the income from my investment portfolio. I focused on the things that were taking my cash flow away and that I was getting no joy from and applied the savings each month toward that goal. Now, I enjoy the mountain cabin and go skiing and mountain biking almost every weekend, and I don't have to worry about the bills getting paid. The monthly income from my investment portfolio takes care of everything.

Okay, enough about me. Here is a story about how my friends Bill and Sandy cut back to move forward. They had graduated from college, were two years into their careers, and pregnant with their first child. Bill had bought a brand-new pickup truck he was super-proud of. It also came with a big payment to be super-proud of. They bought a new house and were experiencing the American Dream—payments, lots of payments, with little left over at the end of the month.

Fast forward a couple of years. Bill still had that big payment on his truck, and they were trying to make ends meet with two successful careers. Bill and Sandy had begun saving a few bucks and were starting to figure out how money works, or in their case, how it wasn't working. You see, in Michigan, it's not only cool to have a big truck, but you also need to have a big boat. Bill and Sandy were beginning to live the lake lifestyle and were around people with nice, shiny boats. A boat was something they knew they wanted, but they hadn't quite figured out how to pay for. And it wasn't just the boat they wanted; it was a lifestyle where they could be on the lake most of the spring and summer, even during workdays, like they had seen some other friends doing. That's an awfully enticing lifestyle. Who wouldn't want to live on a lake with a nice boat, sipping margaritas on your bow while watching the sunset?

Well, for Bill and Sandy, as the old saying goes, if you want something bad enough, you'll figure out a way to get it. These two ended up taking a class on budgeting and personal cash flow management. What they wanted was to pay off all their debt, pay cash for a big boat, and spend as many hours as they could on the lake. They also wanted to save enough money to pay the expenses for the boat all summer long so they did not need to work to support their habit. What an awesome goal it was.

Step-by-step, Bill and Sandy cut their personal expenses, getting rid of every payment except for the mortgage. They sold the truck; they were driving cheap, fuel-efficient cars, and they began to eliminate their cash flow resistance. Money started to pile up, and they bought their first little boat with cash. Bill and Sandy's careers started to take off, and they began to stack up more and more money until they finally had enough to pay for a thirty-one-foot boat they could almost live on. Once that happened, they started putting money in an income-producing securities portfolio to pay the boat's expenses all year-round. But why stop there? At thirty-nine, they finished paying off their house.

These two are debt-free with upper middle-class income and no more bills to pay other than basic utilities, insurance, and food. They are a blast to hang out with. Maybe that's because they're totally free to do as they wish, living on the boat and enjoying life.

Lastly, there are my buddies, John and Steve, two friends who met each other working for a telecom company selling internet access and phone systems to small businesses. These guys had a knack for sales and were doing extremely well. About four or five years into their careers, they had six-figure incomes and were well on their way to becoming corporate executives with all the perks. Both were asked to lead sales teams to pass their skills down to other people and drive the corporation's sales to the next level.

Unfortunately for the company they were working for, John and Steve had a severe dislike for authority. They didn't like being told what to do, and they certainly didn't like having people above them calling the shots who were less talented than they were. Last, but certainly not least, they were making a ton of money for the company but seeing very little of that revenue for themselves. Being the natural rebels they were, they figured they could run their own company and do it better at lower cost and provide more services.

What happened next is the epitome of sacrifice and elimination of unnecessary expenses. Steve was the first to leave the plush corporate job. He started a company selling telecom services to small businesses in direct competition with his former employer. Doing this, Steve's income was cut in half, with even deeper cuts possible if the business didn't take off the way he expected. John followed soon after, but with a baby girl at home, he needed to get a few things in order before he could cut his income in half.

John and Steve both knew the revenue model for selling telecom to small businesses. If that business paid their bills, they got a cut each month for every contract they sold. The more sales they added, the more their monthly income increased. Soon, they added employees and created a sales force that sold many different telecom and software services to small businesses. Within three years, John and Steve had replaced their previous corporate income and created a business worth well into eight figures. At this point, without lifting a finger, they know their bills will be paid and they have a massive recurring income machine that continues to grow as their sales grow.

John and Steve are a blast to hang out with. Part of the fun for them is entertaining people who sell their services and join their team. They both travel all around the world playing the best golf courses, living in the nicest communities, and being husbands and fathers. If they didn't go into work another day, I believe they could sell their business for many millions of dollars and pursue other interests. The thing that fascinates both of them is seeing how big they can grow their business while still enjoying the fruits of their labor. They live the true work-optional lifestyle!

These two examples are not too different from each other. In both situations, the people understood how to create income and what to do with it. John and Steve created a business and Bill and Sandy simply worked with what they had and saved enough money to create income. So, as the story goes, there's more than one way to skin a cat. Either way, the concept to understand here is that income is your single greatest asset. The ability to earn it, make it, and watch it grow are talents that can be honed relatively quickly. The question is: How do you want to build this income, and what do you want it to do for you?

EATING THE ELEPHANT

Take inventory of where you are today. Do you think you can earn and save your way to creating enough income to live a work-optional life? Or could you start a business, sell something, write something, or do something that would create revenue and income that keeps coming in, whether or not you apply effort?

Accumulating enough income to live a work-optional life takes a tremendous amount of money, effort, time, and diligence. It takes a big, meaningful goal to keep you centered on your endgame. You need to set a goal for how much money you would like to have each month and the timeline to accomplish it. Once you do this, you will have a large elephant (goal) that you must eat (accomplish). How do you eat an elephant? One bite at a time.

You see, my friends John and Bill didn't start out with a big opportunity or a massive income they could save to achieve their individual goals. What they did do was decide where they wanted to go and took one bite out of that elephant. What do I mean by that?

John made his first sale to a business that needed internet and phone service. That one sale led to another and another and so on. Bill decided he wanted to be debt-free, so he cut one expense after another after another after another. A few years later, they both looked up to find they had a bunch of money coming in because they had taken one bite at a time.

What one thing can you do today to begin eating the elephant? Is it making one sale? Is it making a phone call? Is it putting a down payment on a rental property? Maybe it's writing your first blog. The key here is to start, get some momentum, and take one small step for yourself.

KEEP STRICT ACCOUNTS

One of my favorite modern philosophers, Jim Rohn, had a unique way of describing the subject of personal accounting. He would ask you to imagine yourself as a corporate executive in charge of a major company. Then imagine you ran that company like you run your personal finances. Would there be a profit each year? Would your stockholders be pleased with your balance sheet? Would more people be interested in investing in the company? Would you even be able to show a balance sheet at the end of the year? In terms of profit, would your investors be impressed to see how much cash you have in the form of savings, your emergency fund, or opportunity funds? Would they be impressed with your bank balance? Last, but certainly not least, would your recurring revenue look good?

This example illustrates that you must know where your money goes! What you focus on will grow, and you must be able to measure your progress toward your work-optional life. The only way to do this is strictly accounting for all of your expenditures and income. Once you've taken one bite of that elephant, you need to know what each bite means in the form of financial reward.

If the subject of keeping track of your finances is lost on you, you're not alone. According to a recent study by US Bank, only 41 percent of Americans use a budget even though it's one of the most effective ways to keep track of finances. This data is only a slight improvement over a 2013 Gallup poll that showed just 32 percent of US households maintain budgets.

Budgeting monthly and tracking your finances have a long way to go in America. For you, doing both is absolutely critical. Imagine yourself as a corporation, and imagine you have to make a call to your shareholders to report your financial results every quarter. You must have something to show them. You must have something to say about what you've been doing over the last three months. We will call this company You, Inc. And its most important shareholder is you.

Put in the most simplistic way possible, is your inflow bigger than your outflow? If you've gotten to the point where your inflow is bigger than your outflow, what are you doing with the difference? Are you using it to produce more income?

I would be remiss if I didn't mention some tools you can use to do this. Quicken is one of the best and oldest software tools out there. Its software will let you measure your net worth and your income and expenses. It is an excellent tool for those who are somewhat computer savvy.

For budgeting and measuring cash flow resistance, EveryDollar.com from the Dave Ramsey corporation is an outstanding tool to track monthly cash flow. One of my favorite things to do with this software is to add a line item in the budget for work-optional lifestyle income. Other popular tools include YNAB (You Need a Budget) and lastly, Mint.com.

In my experience, based on dealing with thousands of budgets for many types of income in many situations over the years, it takes about three months to begin to understand your personal cash flow and build the habit of watching your money. In the third month, budgeting becomes addictive, and you become solely focused on making sure each month has the best outcome possible.

Supporting this idea, according to a study by the University College London psychologist Philippa Lilly, it takes sixty-six days to form a new habit. I questioned the traditional model of a twenty-one-day time frame to create a new habit, as stated by Dr. Maxwell Maltz in his book *Psycho-Cybernetics*. None of the people I've worked with were able to form this new habit within twenty-one days, nor did they build the habit of consistently measuring income and expenses for at least two months. Once you have down the habit of measuring your expenses and income, the maintenance required is only ten minutes per month. Who can't afford to spend ten minutes per month managing their expenses to create a work-optional lifestyle?

If you're not going to track the income and expenses for You, Inc., then your chance of failure is extremely high. You have to know where you are to know where you're going. So please go online right now and sign up for one of the budget tools I mentioned earlier. Then link your bank account and your credit cards to the software and start tracking your monthly income and expenses.

YOU WILL LEND AND NOT BORROW

Now that you're keeping track of your monthly income and expenses, you must also take inventory of what you owe. Any debt you have besides the mortgage on your home is basically unacceptable. Cars depreciate in value; credit card balances that aren't paid each month mean you're struggling with cash flow management and paying 20 percent interest. Student loans are an issue plaguing an incredible number of people who don't have the income to repay them. Remember in Chapter 4 when I asked you to itemize the unnecessary expenses in your life? What I wanted you to do there was to calculate the unnecessary expenses that were taking money away each month. Any debt you have personally beside your mortgage takes money away from you each month.

If you're struggling with debt and find it is taking too much money away from you each month, I recommend Dave Ramsey's *Total Money Makeover* book and his Financial Peace course to get you back on track. The debt snowball process described in his book and courses is the single best and fastest way to pay off debt that I have ever seen. I have helped many of my clients implement this strategy, and I've seen great results. If you have a higher income, you'll have a bigger shovel to dig yourself out of debt, which is all the more reason to generate more income, right? Just think of what you could do if you generated more income and paid off all your debt!

You should start to see progress now as you move through this book. Identify what makes you tick when it comes to money, what it means to you, and what it would mean to work on the things you *want* to work on instead of the things you have to work on. I've encouraged you to earn a little extra income by selling something, doing something, or being something that generates additional cash flow. From there, you want to ensure that you follow strict accounting practices so you can start managing your monthly cash flow. By managing your monthly cash flow, you can start to attack debt and position yourself to really start generating momentum toward your work-optional lifestyle.

With debt, it is better to lend than borrow—if we live a borrowing life, we never get to live the life we really want because we're constantly paying for old mistakes.

FIND YOUR INNER STOIC

Contrary to popular belief, being stoic does not mean being a stone-faced, unemotional robot, no matter the situation, good or bad. In fact, it's practicing a philosophical approach in which you focus on things you can control or have some control over rather than things you cannot control. Do not focus energy on the things you cannot control. This is the stoic mantra called the trichotomy of control. All the strategies I previously mentioned position you financially for a work-optional life and are within your control. That means you should focus all your energy on them. You can control making a budget; you can control your spending. You can also control how much effort you put into generating more monthly income and paying off debt systematically. You cannot control the stock market, the economy, or what has been done in the past.

One of the most famous stoics, Seneca, often lived in poverty even though he was a wealthy man. He did this to prove to himself that even if his wealth were taken away, he still had himself and could deal with misfortune. He also knew with more wealth came more complexity and more to think about. I think most of us can relate this concept to our youth when we didn't have much and were just as happy, if not happier, than we are today. In general, the philosophy of stoicism makes a lot of sense, especially if you are behind on your bills or have too much debt. It may be good to practice being poor for a while to see how you handle it and to build up your resistance so you can build a work-optional life. It's also critical to focus on those things you have some control over and not get too excited about curves in the road when you come to them.

CHALLENGE 5

Which budgeting software are you going to use? Write that down in the space below:

Cash flow software program:

Now, list all of your debts, except your mortgage, from the smallest to largest balance:

1.

2.

3.

Debt and unnecessary expenses are roadblocks to your financial success and your work-optional lifestyle. At this point, you have identified what you want to do with your time when you become work-optional; you have a reason to do it with "chip on your shoulder" mentality. You have found money in your reduction of unnecessary expenses to break through the roadblocks, and with this exercise, you have identified debts that need to be eliminated either with more income or laser-like focus to pay them off. Operate on a monthly budget; use your found money through expense reduction to eliminate all debt except your mortgage. Now we'll move on to Chapter 6, which is where the fun begins!

full
part
time

Chapter 6

KEEP IT SIMPLE

"Simplicity is the ultimate sophistication."

— Leonardo da Vinci

SIMPLIFY EVERYTHING

Maybe you remember the Mel Gibson film *The Patriot*, which debuted in June of 2000. If you haven't seen it, I highly suggest checking it out. The movie portrays a patriot (Gibson) who fights off British soldiers in 1776 to help the war effort and gain independence for the United States. During a scene where British soldiers have his homestead in South Carolina surrounded, Gibson's character Benjamin Taylor asks his sons to recite what he taught them about shooting. The two boys who were about to be in a real firefight say, "Aim small; miss small." Taylor had taught his boys to aim at a small target; that way if they missed, it wouldn't be by much. The same is true for your financial situation; you want to aim small and maintain a minimum number of accounts. The fewer financial accounts you have, the better your chances of finding mistakes and managing your affairs effectively. Then you can keep track of your net worth with ease, and it becomes simple to look for changes in your financial status.

When you look at your personal financial situation, it's important to keep it simple, keep it focused, and keep it neat. Do you have old 401(k)s laying around that you haven't paid attention to in years? Do you have several bank accounts at different banks, but you don't know why?

Over time, we may generate several different accounts for one reason or another. I like to call this "account creep." The older we get, the more accounts we seem to generate.

Sometimes, we open a savings account to get a special rate at a community bank or to get the lowest mortgage interest, but the bank won't finance unless we open an account to make the first payment. It's remarkable how many times I sit down to interview a client who has as many as thirty or forty accounts. How can we possibly keep track of that many accounts and have an accurate picture of our finances?

Banking, lending, and investment institutions are competing for your deposits so they can lend your money to other people in the form of mortgages, lines of credit, business loans, and other types of debt. So from time to time, they like to offer what are called teaser rates to get you to open an account. It seems harmless on the surface, but it can be detrimental to your financial health and clarity over time.

If you're going to live a work-optional life, your finances need to be easy to manage and consolidated. The best way to do this is to have *one* checking account from which you pay all your personal bills. If you are married, it's best if you operate your household out of one joint checking account. It's much easier to track your monthly cash flow this way. If one of you spends too much, it's a good way to get on the same page with your partner about the money you're spending each month.

One checking account can act as the hub for all your financial activities. Part of the reason for "account creep" is the inertia that comes along with automatic bills and the perceived difficulty in changing things around. I ran an experiment a few weeks ago just to see how long it would take to change my bill-pay accounts. Yes, account creep happens to all of us, even your dear author.

In my case, I had a checking account from when I was in high school with a credit line attached, along with a credit card. I had a couple of bills still being paid out of the account, so I just never closed it. Eventually, I was annoyed enough and it took up enough space in my mind to change it. So, I closed three accounts by calling the bank during business hours, and the whole process took twenty-five minutes. Those twenty-five minutes closing accounts and redirecting the automatic bill payments saved me probably four-and-a-half hours of time throughout the rest of my life. Those accounts no longer need to be checked for balances. I don't need to transfer money to them, and I certainly don't want them open and vulnerable to identity theft. Nor would I want them open for my beneficiaries to find after I'm dead, so they have to go through hours of document verification to close them.

You should have only one personal credit card. I'm a strong believer in gaming the system to generate as many free trips and as much credit card swag as possible. One way to do this is to make sure you're maximizing points by having all your household expenses run through one card. If you have more than one card, you have more than one bill to pay, more points to keep track of, and you're likely diluting your benefits.

If you want to get really streamlined (which I suggest), open a credit card through the same bank you have your checking account with, assuming its points system is competitive. That way, you see all your spending activity in one place with one login.

Make sure the bank credit card allows you to transfer your points to most airlines, restaurants, and hotel rewards programs. One great benefit I enjoy is picking which airline I want to use or the hotel I will stay at on my next adventure. A great resource for these programs is The Points Guy at www.thepointsguy.com. Do some research and find out if your bank offers a competitive card with points transfer capability. If you can streamline your accounts this way, you can pay all your bills from one website and manage all your cashflow in one place.

If you're like so many others and carry a balance on your credit card that you can't pay off each month, then don't carry one. Go back to Chapter 5 and use the Dave Ramsey system. Come back debt free—and play the wonderful game of credit card points when you're ready!

Maintain one emergency fund for cash reserves. In Chapter 7, I will go into detail about this type of account and outline why it can also act as your "opportunity fund" if you so choose. For simplification purposes, you should have one emergency fund located in a brokerage account or high yield savings account at your bank or, more preferably, the investment institution you work with for your retirement planning and investments.

Another common mistake I see people make that costs time and heartache is separate savings accounts for everything from travel to braces for the kids. Just have one emergency account, and keep it so full you don't have to worry about the cost of braces or the trip you're going to take. You should be so good at managing your cash flow that you've already built that trip into your monthly budget and most of it will be paid for by credit card points anyway.

Your emergency fund should be set up to cover things you cannot plan for monthly, such as braces, a broken windshield, or a faulty hot water heater. Get rid of the small accounts, and get serious about budgeting and simplification. This will save you time, which is the most valuable resource you have in focusing on your work-optional life plan. As your plan expands, so will your emergency/opportunity fund.

Maintain two retirement accounts per individual. If you have a full-time job, the probability is high that you have a 401(k), 403(b), or other retirement plan you contribute to, either to get the employer match or because you've implemented the "wait and hope" plan I described earlier in this book. Either way, you should only have one of these accounts, and it should only be with your current employer. All other retirement plans should be consolidated into an IRA (individual retirement account), which would be your other retirement account for a total of two.

If you're married, you cannot comingle your retirement accounts with your spouse, so that will mean four retirement accounts maximum per household. The only exception to this rule would be if you have Roth assets that were either in a Roth 401(k) or Roth IRA. If that is the case, you would have three per person maximum at all times.

Not only is it a good idea for you to keep your finances simple, but it's also a good idea to simplify your accounts to benefit your loved ones. Imagine the unthinkable has happened—you stepped off the curb on your way to work and got hit by a bus. Just like that, your spouse has lost their partner and your kids have lost a parent. You knew your money was spread out, but you had more important things to do. If you're like many clients I see, you probably had anywhere from ten to thirty different savings, checking, brokerage, and retirement accounts. Your spouse or kids are left sorting out the mess you left behind because I'm also quite sure nobody knows where everything is, and some of those accounts may not have had a beneficiary or transfer on death designation. Your family is left waiting for statements to come in the mail or for creditors to call asking for payment. Even worse, you get notices that some of these accounts have been escheated to the state. This is what I would call a sub-optimal outcome.

WHAT YOU FOCUS ON WILL GROW

I think I've made the point that it pays to keep things simple by limiting the number of accounts you have. It also pays to have everything consolidated with as few institutions as possible. I highly recommend aggregating all your financial assets using online tools to consolidate information from many financial accounts in one convenient place. These tools can track your bank, brokerage, checking, retirement, mortgage, and credit cards using one login and let you and whomever you trust see all that you have, updated in real time in one location. If you're married, it's extremely helpful for your partner to be able to see everything, just in case something happens. If you're not married, a couple of trusted individuals should have the password and login information. That way, they can unfold your financial situation in case catastrophe strikes. Some examples of aggregation tools you can use are Quicken, Mint, and E-Money. Several similar apps can be found on your smartphone.

Based on the information we just went through, below is an example of how things should look. I'll illustrate the account map for a married couple who owns a home with a mortgage and has two incomes. I'll also illustrate an account map for a single individual who owns their own home.

Married Couple (maximum of ten accounts)

One Joint Bank Checking Account
Four Retirement Accounts (two employer-sponsored retirement plans and two IRAs)

- Two Roth IRAs if you have these accounts

One Mortgage
One Joint Cash Reserve/Opportunity Account
One Joint Credit Card (to maximize point values)

Single Person (maximum of eight accounts)

One Checking Account
Two Retirement Accounts (one employer-sponsored retirement plan and one IRA)

- One Roth IRA can be added

One Mortgage
One Cash Reserve/Opportunity Account

One Credit Card (to maximize point values)

Of course, these examples do not cover all the situations you may find yourself in, especially if you own rental houses and/or run your own business. Each of those entities should have separate accounts attached to them. If that is the case for you, it's imperative to use the account aggregation tools mentioned earlier so you can see all your riches in one location, whether they are business-related or personal.

THE MONEY COMPACTOR

After you've consolidated your financial picture, a very interesting thing begins to happen. I call it the "Money Compactor" effect. It describes when your focus becomes small and you're able to see changes over time in your net worth. Then you can act with more decisiveness because you begin to understand how all the little things you do affect the whole picture financially. You can begin to see how much income your portfolio is producing and begin to quantify what it will be able to pay for. You can add up your income from various resources and see how you're progressing toward your income goal. You can see your net worth change over time.

Then the mental games begin. You'll want to get your numbers just a little higher to the next round number. This is the mental game we play with ourselves known as "hedonic adaptation." We become comfortable with the level we've reached and want more. Having a narrow focus feeds this beast, and our wealth grows faster than it would without having this groundwork done.

Simplify and consolidate your financial accounts. Your family will thank you, and I'm certain you will build wealth faster.

CHALLENGE 6

This one should be easy! Count how many open accounts you have at all lending, banking, and investment institutions. This includes bank accounts, credit cards, auto loans, student loans, 401(k)s, IRAs etc. Let's see if you can add all of them up!

Write the number here:

Now, calculate how many accounts above need to be closed or consolidated with other accounts.

Write that number here:

When will you have this process completed? In going through this process, think about the time it might take for a family member to find all these accounts if something happens to you. Perhaps that is good motivation to get it done now. Simplify your financial picture so you can keep your focus small!

full
part
time

Chapter 7

THE SUPER RESERVE

"I'd like to live as a poor man with lots of money."

— Pablo Picasso

CASH EQUALS OPPORTUNITY

Mark Cuban, the billionaire owner of the Dallas Mavericks and star of ABC's *Shark Tank*, said it best in his now infamous blog post about having cash on the sidelines:

> The first step to getting rich is having cash available. You aren't saving for retirement. You are saving for the moment you need cash. Buy and hold is a sucker's game for you. This market is a perfect example. Right at the very moment when cash creates unbelievable opportunity, those that followed the buy and hold strategy have no cash.... Cash is king for those wanting to get rich.

I couldn't agree more.

At this point, you've hopefully learned a few things. You've learned how to eliminate unnecessary expenses, get out of debt, simplify your finances, and most importantly, you've found a reason to change your money habits. We are now on the precipice of your plan to develop the income you need for your version of a work-optional life. I'm not preparing you for the kind of life where you do nothing and sit on a beach, but the kind of life where every day is a new adventure. Every day can be a new calling to something that piques your interests. At the very least, every day can now be less stressful because you're designing a plan to have a few extra dollars flowing into your life each month. You've now laid the groundwork for some serious financial success, and this chapter is the fuel to add to your fire. The steps I've outlined leading up to this point are crucial, but the concept of having a super reserve of cash is the single most important step you can take to gain financial independence.

Now that you've cleaned up "You, Inc." from a financial standpoint and you have no debt except your house, you can begin the journey. Since you identified an amount of income you'd like to have coming in the door each month in Chapter 5, here is your catalyst for success. You want to have as much cash saved as you can possibly stand. This means not contributing to anything except your cash reserve until your goal is met. Don't start your 401(k)—don't start investing in anything. Just save cash every month until your choking on it.

Traditional advice tells us all to save three to six months' worth of income in an emergency fund at the bank. While that is nice, general advice to the masses, it doesn't give you a distinct financial advantage. That money philosophy never made anyone rich. If it did, you would hear things like, "That six months of emergency reserves really changed my life." You don't hear that because it's boring, old financial advice that doesn't work in the real world. Saving for a rainy day is what our grandparents told us to do. Let's face it, Grandma and Grandpa were not that exciting.

Because of this rainy-day advice and boring money philosophy, I'd like to flip the script. Saving cash is not for a rainy day. Having an emergency savings account is one of the most boring things I've ever had to coach my clients on. In fact, one of my clients helped me to change my view of this advice. My client and I were sitting down having coffee to discuss one of his latest business ideas, of which he had many. As his advisor, I felt one of the ideas he was describing had some value and could be profitable if he acted quickly. I also mentioned that I liked his business idea because it didn't take much cash to start up.

He went on to vet other ideas that would have needed a bunch of cash to start up and the right people and circumstances to fall into place. I felt he didn't have the means to make those ideas happen. I told him I felt his cash reserves were insufficient to execute his more expensive idea. What he said next changed my philosophy on emergency accounts. He said, "So what you mean is I need to have an opportunity account, instead of an emergency account, when these ideas come up?" That brilliant choice of words would forever change how I viewed cash reserves and how I helped my clients reimagine the old-fashioned emergency fund.

After that discussion, I never recommended emergency savings again. Instead, I recommended setting up an opportunity fund that could double as an emergency account in the unlikely event it was needed. I started recommending my clients save obscene amounts of cash so that both opportunities and emergencies could be handled from one place. This became known as a "super reserve" and changed the wealth trajectory for almost everyone who implemented it.

We went on to design a three-tier super reserve so it would begin to compound on itself over time. The three-tier super reserve would also have the potential to earn much more than the bank would offer for a savings account. More details on this to follow.

HOW MUCH

How much should you have in your super reserve? The answer is almost certainly—more! All kidding aside, it's important to know how much money your three-tier super reserve should have and how you should situate that hard-earned cash. Since you're not contributing to a 401(k) at this point and you've eliminated debt except your mortgage, it's all hands on deck to build up your super reserve. How much depends on what you do for a living, if you own rental properties, and if you run your own business. So, I'll break it down by how you're employed and if you have rental properties.

If you are employed by someone else and earn a regular paycheck, the super reserve amount to aim for should start at six months' worth of expenses. You simply multiply your monthly expenses by six. For example, if your monthly expenses are $4,000, you should have $24,000 in your three-tier super reserve. I know that sounds like a lot of money, but if you've followed the steps laid out in this book so far, you should be able to build up the cash within eighteen to twenty-four months. Remember, all of your debt is paid off, you're operating on a monthly budget, and you've simplified your finances.

Once you've amassed this dollar amount, you'll want to structure it into three equal parts or tiers. The first tier should be saved in a liquid money market mutual fund in a brokerage account. A brokerage account can be set up online through Fidelity, TD Ameritrade, Charles Schwab, or E-Trade for virtually no cost. This account acts much like a bank account, except you can buy stocks, bonds, and mutual funds. You can set up an automatic monthly contribution to this account directly from your joint or personal checking account. If you have a trusted financial advisor, they can usually set this up for you as well, but your costs will be higher because they are doing the leg work by establishing the account and setting up the contributions.

Your second tier will reside in a short-term bond fund that will produce a higher return over time than the money market fund, but still be relatively safe from value fluctuations. These short-term bond mutual funds pay a monthly income called a dividend. You'll want that dividend to be reinvested each month to buy more shares of the fund, which, in turn, will produce more income each month. You will need to call the firm where your brokerage account is held, search online, or ask your financial advisor for help identifying a good mutual fund in this category. There should be no significant charge to get in or out of this fund. In other words, it needs to be completely liquid, which means you can sell it for cash at any time.

Now your three-tier super reserve begins to build on itself. And you have $8,000 in a money market mutual fund and $8,000 in a short-term bond mutual fund paying dividends each month, adding to the balance without your effort or time.

Next, you're going to want to take some risk and add the last tier to your three-tier super reserve. This will be known as the high-yield tier, which carries with it some risk to the funds you're saving but a high degree of monthly income in the form of dividends. I know this is not your traditional advice, but how has that been working for you?

In this section of your super reserve, it's time to take some risk. This is where we would want to buy a high-yield bond mutual fund. Your dividends on this fund should be 5 percent or more per year. You will not worry about value fluctuations here because you already have four months' worth of reserves that will not move up and down in value very much and can be liquidated at a moment's notice. This last tier is where all the magic begins to happen, and your super reserve begins to build on itself more quickly. You now have six months of income put away in a super reserve and adding to itself each month through monthly dividends that are being reinvested without any effort on your part.

To summarize this concept, we've identified the steps necessary to get to this point. You have no debt except for your house, you will have simplified your finances, and you have become ultra-focused on your monthly budget. If you've gotten to the six-month mark with your super reserve and situated your funds the way I described earlier, it's time to set some bigger goals! This is where you decide how big you want your super reserve to be and what you want it to pay for. Anything saved beyond the six-month amount is now going to contribute to your work-optional lifestyle. The account should look something like the following based on our $4,000 per month expense model:

- $8,000 money market fund (making 1 to 2 percent)
- $8,000 short-term bond fund (making 2 to 4 percent paying monthly dividends)
- $8,000 high-yield bond fund (making 3 to 8 percent paying monthly dividends)

If structured like the model above, this reserve account should be producing at least $50 a month in additional deposits through reinvested dividends. Those dividends buy more shares, and those shares produce more dividends. Your super reserve begins to fund itself with compound cash flow and grows without your effort. That may not pay a lot of bills, but it's a heck of a good start. This super reserve also gives you the security of knowing that whatever you decide to do or whatever happens to you in the workplace, you're okay for at least six months. That kind of peace of mind is priceless, and it allows you to focus your energy on creativity, family, and other options for making money.

The question from here is how far you're willing to take this? Some people stop right here, satisfied with knowing they have a little extra income every month. Some people keep going, building up enough super reserve to pay all their monthly bills using dividends. Others took the reserves they built beyond the six-month requirement and started rental real estate businesses or used the funds to buy a business they always wanted.

Let's use my sister as an example. She built up enough super reserve to live on for three years. The key to her success is that every time she built up enough cash beyond her six-month requirement, she put a down payment on a rental property. This went on for almost ten years. By the time it was all over, and she had sold most of her rentals, she was sitting on a massive pile of cash. She then decided to buy a car wash with about $65,000 she had accumulated through the sale of her rental properties. That car wash now generates about $40,000 in income per year. She will earn her money back in a couple of years and have that cash flow for many years to come. As of right now, she's working on automating the operation so she doesn't have to be there. Talk about a work-optional lifestyle! She really enjoys operating this business. It's a low effort, low overheard operation that creates a good income and allows her freedom to focus on the next activity she desires to put effort into. The key to her success was taking her excess cash and investing it into rental real estate and a car wash.

Now, that's a good story, and certainly one to imitate if your desire is to own rental real estate, which I will get into in Chapter 9. The magic happens when you've devoted yourself to focusing on this one goal of having six months of expenses saved in your super reserve. This starts the waterfall of good financial opportunities because you finally have the cash to take advantage of them. At this point in the process, you've focused on only one goal, which was to build this reserve.

WHAT WILL IT PAY FOR?

We now know that six months is the bare minimum and that the funds will produce dividends and grow without your effort. It's time to figure out how far to go with this. You must make this decision prior to doing anything else with your money. Here are some ideas that might be helpful:

1. Leave it at six months and watch it grow.
2. Save up enough money to put a down payment on a rental property.
3. Keep building the fund, ignoring all other traditional savings strategies, and invest the money as financial opportunities come up.
4. Save up more to support the purchase of a small business.
5. Build the fund so much that the dividends pay your monthly bills, and you can quit your day job in search of more meaningful activities.
6. Diversify your emergency reserve by building a bigger portfolio of stock mutual funds or index funds, or buy individual stocks.
7. Reinvest the dividends into a college fund for your kids.

As you can see, with the options laid out, there are myriad ways to use this concept. This process is the very cornerstone of building wealth and gives you ultimate flexibility in what you can do with the money. Old school advice tells us to invest in our 401(k) and save up three months' worth of expenses in case of an emergency. My strategy gives you the ability to do what you want to do with your money and doesn't confine you to a wait and hope approach designed by the Federal Government. Don't get me wrong—I like what government can do for a society, but when it comes to managing money, I'll let the record speak for itself. There are record deficits and debt, and our Social Security system is broke. I'm not so sure I'd plan my future based on what they give me.

That said, as long as you've gotten to this step and completed it, you're better off than 60 percent of your friends. According to a bankrate.com survey, 60 percent of Americans can't afford to pay $1,000 for an unexpected expense. It's really not their fault. The Federal Government and the financial community never thought to set up an employer-sponsored payroll deduction emergency savings plan. Instead, they tell you to tackle multiple goals at the same time with money you don't really know if you have. The common advice I see out there is to split contributions between your 401(k) and your emergency fund. On this plan, you'd fund your super reserve and nothing else until you get to the six-month mark. Setting it up the way I described earlier will allow it to feed itself each month and grow without your effort.

Now it's time to address the good old 401(k). If you've gotten this far, you have my permission to put this book down and go back to taking traditional financial advice. You can now begin making 401(k) contributions and participating in the wait and hope plan. You now have permission to save 10 to 15 percent of your income in the 401(k) and receive your employer match if there is one. Alternatively, and/or simultaneously, you can choose to continue reading and start building some serious wealth and some serious work-optional income. So, which will it be—the wait and hope plan, the work-optional plan, or both? If you've come this far, my guess is you're not the type of person who just goes with the flow.

It would be silly for me to suggest leaving money on the table now that you've built your super reserve. For example, if your employer matches 3 percent of your contributions, you should contribute at least 3 percent. Take the free money and invest in growth stock funds or stock index funds for the long term. You're going to be doing some very interesting things with the rest of your excess income in the chapters ahead.

(See the Challenge on the next page)

CHALLENGE 7

Write down the amount you will need in your super reserve. Add up your monthly expenses and multiply that amount by 6. Then set a goal for when your super reserve will be obtained using the excess money you've created in your monthly budget by getting rid of debt and unnecessary expenses.

My Super Reserve will be $_________ by ________ (month/year). I will save $______ every month until I get there.

Take action by setting up the account and sending the amount above automatically each month to be invested. Be sure to seek guidance if you are unsure of how to set up the three-tier reserve correctly. You will invest in the money market fund for the first tier, in the short-term bond fund for the second tier, and lastly, you will build the third tier with the high yield bond fund.

full
part
time

Chapter 8

FIND YOUR NUMBER

"Imagination is the beginning of creation, you imagine what you desire, you will what you imagine, and at last you create what you will."

— George Bernard Shaw

WHAT IS IT?

In Chapter 1's challenge, you listed five things you would do if you were living a work-optional lifestyle. In this chapter, we're going to discuss how to define the dollar amount you need to make your desire a reality. Many different formulas can be used to come up with that number, but we're going to focus on one distinct way to calculate it.

Since you've been reading every chapter and hopefully you've been magnetized to every word I have written, you know that income is the outcome. If you built your three-tier super reserve, you already have income coming in without your effort. I intentionally designed the formula for the three-tier reserve to help people realize they can build an income stream; however small it may be. Now your job is to figure out how big your income is going to be and what it's going to pay for to allow you to live your work-optional lifestyle.

If your goal is to produce enough income to pay all of your basic expenses, then we figure out what that number is and use our work-optional formula to create the income. Perhaps your goal is to replace the monthly income of your spouse so they can focus their creative energy elsewhere. Perhaps you just want your mortgage to be paid so you can drop to working part-time and spend more time with your kids. The key is to break down the number you need into a monthly amount and work backward. For now, my job is to get you to identify the monthly income that will set you free, or partially free to do what you are intended to do.

In my first example, I'm going to paint a picture of the average American Joe who works hard, has read this book up to this point, and has created a six-month super reserve. Joe would like to have enough money each month to pay his mortgage without having to apply his time and effort to pay for that mortgage. To keep the numbers easy, let's say his monthly mortgage is $1,000 per month. In fact, according to lendingtree.com, the average monthly nationwide mortgage payment is $1,049. So, maybe this example pertains to more people than not.

Joe knows this number of $1,000 per month will help him change his career to operating the fly-fishing guide service he's always imagined.

When he attached meaning to his money in Chapter 1, fly-fishing was at the top of his list of things he wanted to do. Let's say his super reserve is already generating $50 per month. He's already 5 percent funded toward his goal, and all he's done at this point is set up his super reserve. Joe likes the concept of saving his money and producing monthly dividends from that savings.

The formula for achieving Joe's desire to have his super reserve pay $1,000 per month toward his mortgage is to take that monthly amount and multiply it by 250. Then, voilà, we have his number! Joe needs to have $1,000/month of income to pay his mortgage so he can afford to earn less income for a short time while he gets his fly-fishing business under way: $1,000 x 250 = $250,000. This is the lump sum Joe needs to have in the high yield portion of his reserve to accomplish his work-optional goal. Joe is willing to accept some risk in his investments to achieve that desired income. I will get more specific on the details of this income and which instruments can deliver your outcome in Chapter 9.

Joe is never going to retire because he loves his job and he loves being on the water helping people become better fishermen. His mortgage is being paid for, so he only has to make do for his basic expenses once he jumps off to start his fly-fishing adventure. He knows he can cover the rest of his expenses by simply becoming a guide working for another company, or as a contractor booking trips on his own. Joe goes the contractor route and begins to build a reputation as an outstanding angler. He begins booking many private client trips with wealthy business owners who like his sense of humor and whom he puts in a position to catch fish every time. Joe's business starts to take off, and now he has more trips booked than he can handle. His website is also beginning to generate new clients.

Now, here's where it gets extremely fun. Joe is able to bring on some guides underneath him and show them the tricks he's learned over the past few years. Each guide pays him a booking fee per trip. His business is now growing with less and less personal effort from him. Joe is being asked for interviews by fly-fishing magazine and the business goes viral. Joe is now earning enough money from the guides underneath him that he no longer needs to be a guide himself. He even hires a lead guide to take over the operation and oversee all guiding activities. Joe is living his dream, and now he has the option to keep guiding, step back, or continue to grow his operation. Over the years, he found peace in tying the flies he would use on the river with his clients. He now spends about half his time tying flies and the other half working with clients through his business. For Joe, every day brings in peace and happiness. He's doing exactly what he wants to do now instead of what he has to do. That is the definition of a work-optional lifestyle. Joe gets up every day with a choice. He chose to build his super reserve first and focused solely on that goal. Had his money been tied up in a 401(k), this vision would never have been realized.

In my next example, we have Stella. Stella has been married to Mike for a few years, and she worked for a marketing company full-time. Mike was doing quite well in his career, but they both had a nagging feeling they would someday like to get out of the grind. Stella has a particular interest in real estate since her father became quite wealthy operating little rental properties here and there and small apartment complexes. Stella and Mike knew they had to get out of debt, paying off everything except for their house. They also knew they had to build a super reserve so one day they could buy a rental property that would eventually help them rise above the fray. Their initial goal was to have $1,000 per month coming in from real estate. Between Stella and Mike, they made about $90,000 a year. They knew that six months of expenses equaled about $40,000. They saved over three years and finally hit their six-month super reserve goal of $40,000.

This was a tremendous accomplishment for Stella and Mike. They got so addicted to watching their super reserve grow that they just decided to keep going. Over the next two years, they saved another $25,000 and their super reserve ballooned to $65,000, producing regular monthly dividends. During that time, Stella studied for and passed the state real estate exam. Stella knew if they put part of their super reserve money to work, they'd be able to buy their first rental property and create some additional monthly income. Their strategy was to have Stella purchase the property with her license and put her real estate commission back into the property to improve it. This would make it more desirable and create the potential for even more monthly income.

Within six months of Stella passing her real estate exam, she joined a local real estate brokerage while keeping her day job so she could search properties and learn from some of the other brokers. Stella and Mike's super reserve was at $70,000, and they knew they were ready to invest in their first rental property. They just had to find the right one. At this point, Stella and Mike had $30,000 more than what they needed in their six-month super reserve—that was going to be their down payment.

After a few months of intense searching, Stella finally found the right property. It was a three-bedroom, two bath, single-family home that was coming out of foreclosure. This property hit the market at $87,000 but needed a lot of work. The mortgage payment on this home was going to be $600 per month with taxes and insurance. Stella knew they could rent the property for $1,600 per month. This essentially meant that their earnings on the property each month would be $1,000. Stella and Mike decided to pull the trigger and buy the house. They made an $8,700 down payment and used the rest of the savings to rehab the home. Things were touch and go while the property was being rehabilitated. Two months later, they had a renter and a twelve-month lease. The first year they made $12,000 in rental income after expenses.

Over the next three years, Stella and Mike would continue to collect rent and keep the same tenant in the property. They accumulated another $30,000 in that period and were prepared to add another property to their growing real estate empire. After a total of seven years, Stella and Mike were able to accumulate two triplexes and one single family home. The net rental income on those properties grew to $5,000 per month! Stella could quit her day job and focus on her family and successful real estate business while Mike continued in his career.

I want to take a moment to reflect on these last two examples. What did they both have in common? The obvious answer is they had laser-like focus on building their super reserve. Secondly, they both took four to seven years to get to a place where they had some freedom to do what truly gave them meaning. That means there is no shortcut, only perseverance and developing an addiction to saving money in your super reserve. Living your financial life this way gives you the freedom to live your life as you choose.

These two examples are very closely correlated to actual situations I've helped coach my clients through using the super reserve philosophy. Finally, both subjects in these examples took some risk. Joe took the risk of trying a new career and Stella and Mike took the risk of buying a rental property that might go vacant for a few months at a time. If you take these risks, an inherent chance exists that you will lose financially. In both cases, however, the super reserve was there to back them up if things went wrong.

My last example carries the greatest risk and also the greatest reward.

Henry was in his mid-forties and had been working for a large IT services corporation. He and a colleague from work started engaging in some part-time IT consulting for small professional businesses on the side. Henry knew he didn't want to work for a big corporation forever. He enjoyed the freedom and excitement of running his own business doing IT consulting. His main goal was to replace his cushy $150,000 annual salary. The only problem was he didn't have the cash to jump off and start his own thing.

Henry consulted his financial advisor, who was recommended by a close friend. He asked his advisor to weigh in on his starting his own business. Henry's advisor recommended he stop making all retirement plan contributions, get on a budget, and save at least $25,000 so if he fell short in his new venture, he could still pay his bills for a few months while he sought new employment.

The other issue they discussed was his partnership with the colleague. Henry and his potential partner didn't see eye to eye about the direction of this burgeoning business. Henry's partner wanted to keep the business small and continue to work on it as a permanent side hustle with the IT job as a backstop. Henry wanted to expand the business and use his creativity to attract clients and build a sustainable revenue stream that would allow him to exit the corporate world. Henry eventually decided to buy out his partner. Henry did not have the cash to do this, but he knew if some new customers came on, he could easily survive. This was a big risk, and the partner was more than happy to take a small buyout and run. Henry arranged for a small business loan of $100,000 and paid out his now former partner. He was then free to run the business as he saw fit.

Next, Henry brought on several new customers and the business started cranking. Fast forward two years—the business was doing $1.5 million in revenue with $200,000 in take-home pay for Henry. He also purchased a new building to house his business. Currently, Henry keeps $25,000 for his personal super reserve, which isn't much compared to the $90,000 he has in his business super reserve. He's going to lease his building to other small businesses to offset his costs and continue to expand on his operations. He's gotten the entrepreneurial bug and has several other businesses he's in the early stages of forming.

Henry's financial advisor recently asked him when he planned to retire. Henry's response was interesting. He said he wanted to, in his words, "Maybe slow down a little bit by age seventy, but if I still feel good and energized, I'll just keep going."

In just a few years, Henry had broken free of the idea of retirement, built up some cash, and started to live the life he had envisioned. What's more interesting is he was never looking to retire in a traditional sense. He was living his life on purpose, and working on his business was a vital part of who he was. Essentially, he was having fun every day doing his thing—what a concept! That is a part of the essence of a work-optional lifestyle—having fun and living your life on purpose.

Henry's primary source of income is his business. He has a super reserve between his business and personal account of $115,000, and that is sufficient for his needs. After observing Henry for a couple of years, that number may be a little smaller than it could be because Henry has a propensity to enter into new business ventures from time to time. Of course, his basic needs can be met for six months no matter what else happens. We'll have to see where his business and new ideas take him.

What these three stories have in common, as mentioned earlier, is that each person stuck to the formula to achieve their super reserve. The next step they took was based on a purpose or particular interest they had that happened to generate some income, and they defined what that income needed to be. That purpose and the corresponding income led to a financial situation that provided a work-optional lifestyle.

Maybe you don't have a particular interest. That's definitely okay. But something might grab you along the way on your journey, and it's better to be ready for it financially when it comes. Even if it never comes and you have a super reserve feeding itself income every month, at least you can be secure in knowing your financial needs are met in your "real life" and that an emergency or large expense won't financially derail you. Who knows? Maybe you will just keep building it, and one day it will start producing enough income that you can work half time or not at all.

The point here is to define two things: What interests you that could generate income, and how much income would you like it to generate each month?

CHALLENGE 8

Write down how much income you would like to generate each month to live your work-optional life and when you would like to achieve that goal.

Monthly Income Amount:

Date I would like to achieve this goal:

Which of the examples (Joe, Stella and Mike, or Henry) did you like the most? If you gravitated to one story over another, chances are a similar path might be right for you. Remember, if you're doing what you love, you will never work another day in your life. In the next chapter, we'll expand on this idea and give you more resources to generate this income.

full
part
time

Chapter 9

TRIANGULATE

"If you don't find a way to make money while you sleep, you will work until you die."

— Warren Buffett

INCOME IS FREEDOM

I love the above quote from Warren Buffet, not only because of its utter truth but because it begs the question, "How do we make money while we sleep?" Most of us are brought up in environments where, for the most part, we are told we must labor for money—to put time and effort into making money.

When you are first starting out, that is true; you must earn money through labor, time, and effort. Once you have found a way to make money with your labor, time, and effort, however, the trick is to use one of three methods to begin harnessing the power of that money to make more money while you sleep. The focus of this chapter is the three ways you can make money while you sleep. There may be more ways, but in my research, these three make up 90 percent of the options in the real world.

In Chapter 8, I asked you to identify which of my quasi real-life examples you gravitated to the most: Joe, Stella and Mike, or Henry. Which one did you pick? Now I'm going to lay out the advantages and disadvantages of each approach and what you need to do to start on these three paths to your work-optional life.

As a graphic representation, I'd like you to envision what I call the income triangle. This triangle shows the three ways to make money while you sleep. It may make it easier for you to pick which type of income source works for you. At the top of the triangle is completely passive income, which requires almost zero time to maintain, no physical labor, and makes money no matter what you do. On either vertex of the bottom part of the triangle you have semi-passive and active income. As those names imply, semi-passive income requires some time and physical effort to make money while you sleep, and active income requires a lot of time and effort to make money while you sleep.

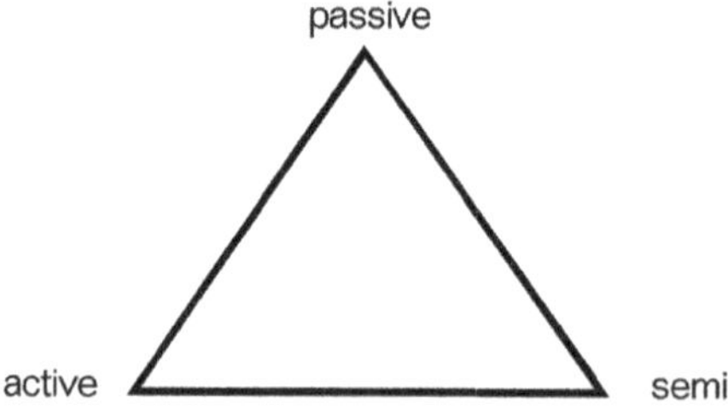

Passive income is at the top of the triangle because it should be part of everyone's plan, and it can lead you to the two other apexes of the triangle by providing enough cash to start an active or semi-active income plan. When you create your super reserve, this is the *de facto* outcome of the process. If you built your super reserve as I suggested in Chapter 7, you are already receiving passive income through the dividends paid each month on the securities or funds you own in that account. This requires no effort from you after establishing the reserve and selecting your investments. The dividends compound on themselves, and you go to sleep each night knowing, just as the sun rises in the morning, your funds will pay those dividends and continue to grow your super reserve without any additional time or effort from you. This is the very definition of passive income. No effort and no time are the hallmark of this work-optional life strategy.

One drawback is the amount of cash it takes to live your work-optional life on this strategy. It will take more of your own money and a lot of time for dividends to accumulate to a point where you can meet your number. If you can remember from Joe's example in Chapter 8, he needed $250,000 of his own money to make the jump from where he was to where he wanted to go. He needed $1,000 per month to take care of his basic expenses so he could follow his passion.

PASSIVE INCOME

There are four pillars to passive income that will make up the foundation of your passive income strategy. If you can remember the formula for achieving the monthly income you desire, it's the amount you wish to receive every month multiplied by 250. For example, if I want $2,000 per month of completely passive income, then I need to multiply that by 250, which equals $500,000. As I said before, this requires a lot of time and savings.

From there, I want to split that amount up into the four pillars of passive income, which are:

1. Dividend-paying stocks
2. REITS (real estate investment trusts)
3. MLPs (master limited partnerships)
4. High-yield municipal bonds

Divided in quarters, this mix will help you achieve your income goal. Before I describe each type of investment, it's important to know there are risks associated with each method I will describe, and there will be ups and downs in the market for each one of these securities. However, the income distributions should be consistent if done correctly.

Dividend-Paying Stocks: These are by far one of the best-understood ways to generate passive income. Basically, you invest in shares of a public company that pays its profits to shareholders in the form of quarterly dividends. Generally, these companies are some of the best to invest in because they return their hard-earned cash to shareholders. Many financial planners and online brokerages offer ETFs (exchange traded funds) and mutual funds to invest broadly into many different companies in one investment. These options diversify your risk and generally require a low initial investment. An added bonus of using a mutual fund or ETF is they can pay dividends monthly, which is critical for your overall plan. I suggest you research large company dividend funds using your advisor or online brokerage provider. Large US companies offer the most stability and financial strength so those dividends will be there for the long haul.

REITS (Real Estate Investment Trusts): These consist of publicly traded real estate companies that buy commercial real estate and rent it to large corporate tenants. The stocks of these real estate companies are traded daily on the open market. These stocks distribute 90 percent of the rent received to shareholders like you and me. This is a great way to own real estate without having to take out a mortgage, change a light-bulb, or plunge a toilet.

There are thousands of variations of these investments in the marketplace. The basic idea here is that whatever you buy needs to yield around 5 percent annually to the shareholder. If I invest $10,000 into the REIT, it should pay me about $500 per year in dividends. That is a 5 percent yield. Most online brokerage houses can point you in the right direction, and of course, any good financial planner can help with this as well. Ideally, you earn 5 percent in dividends per year and the investment should have a five year or longer track record of good performance relative to its peers.

MLPs (Master Limited Partnerships): These are the next pillar of your passive income strategy. Similar to REITS, these investments pay monthly income to the investor in the form of dividends, passing most of the cash they earn onto the end investor. Unlike REITS, these investments are far more volatile and typically pay higher income to the investor in exchange for that volatility. MLPs are publicly listed limited partnerships that trade on the open market just like REITS. Most MLPs have general partners and many have limited partners (the investors). The general partners manage the operations, while the limited partners purchase shares in the MLP and provide capital in return for cash distributions from the entity's operations. These MLPs primarily exist in the energy and energy infrastructure businesses. Many different types of MLPs exist, my favorite being pipeline MLPs that transport natural gas and crude oil. The annual yield from these investments averages 7.7 percent according to Kiplinger.com. This means for every $10,000 invested, you may receive up to $770 per year in dividend income.

MLPs come with some tax advantages you cannot get from owning a diversified mutual fund or ETF (exchange traded fund). I suggest using the fund as opposed to the individual MLPs because many funds pay monthly income. As I said before, you can consult almost any online brokerage, or your personal financial planner for resources on which one to use, but make sure they provide monthly dividends.

Municipal Bonds: These securities round out the final pillar of your passive income strategy. Municipal bonds typically pay federally tax-free interest in exchange for their purchase. A municipality needs to issue a bond to fund new runways and facilities to accommodate a growing population. You, as the investor, can purchase a bond for $1,000 to give them the money to start their project. In exchange, that municipality will pay you interest twice a year from their revenue until that bond matures in a few years. At that time, they will give you back your money, and you can reinvest or move it to a different investment vehicle.

For the purpose of your work-optional life strategy, you will want to purchase high-yield municipal bonds for this part of your strategy through the use of a mutual fund or ETF (exchange traded fund). High-yield municipal bonds typically have lower credit worthiness and are more volatile than the rest of the options in this category. By using a mutual fund or ETF, you diversify your risk and give the experts the ability to select appropriate bonds for you. Most funds pay monthly income, which is critical to this plan. Please consult your personal financial planner or an online brokerage to help you with this investment strategy.

Using these four pillars as your passive-income strategy provides you with the income needed each month to explore your work-optional life. Ideally, you would have a quarter of your money invested equally in each strategy we discussed. The annual yield on your portfolio must be at least 5 percent and preferably 6 percent for the formula to work. That means the portfolio must maintain that income every year, and you have to monitor it for fluctuations in dividend payments and market value. This is not foolproof; nothing is, and it must be cared for and maintained just like anything else. Consult your financial professional and/or your online brokerage provider to determine the specific strategies to implement. This is a fully passive strategy that will make money while you sleep and generate monthly cash flow sufficient to meet your goals based on the formula we've been using.

The last point I'll make about the four pillars of passive income is they are not the only pillars available. Some other examples of completely passive income would be preferred stocks, covered calls, unit investment trusts, and bond mutual funds and ETFs. The ones I've mentioned here tend to produce the highest monthly income. I don't recommend flying blind on this, so seek counsel from a good certified financial planner if you do not know what you're doing or don't trust the online brokerage system to produce the needed result. In many cases, you may be able to pay a professional for their best recommendations at an hourly rate or project cost. Some advisors will charge you based on a percentage of the assets they manage in your portfolio.

SEMI-PASSIVE INCOME

Semi-passive income is income you must put some effort into to create. The best example of semi-passive income is owning a single-family home as a rental property. I can't tell you how many times owning a rental home has been misrepresented as passive income, especially by those real estate people who claim it is the be-all and end-all strategy for financial success. The truth is every physical piece of real estate needs maintenance and upkeep, which you have to do or pay to have done. However, adding this strategy to your work-optional life is fairly lucrative if done correctly.

The passive part of this strategy is simple. There may be long stretches of time when a property is running itself fairly well, and you don't need to put effort into fixing it, finding a new tenant, or collecting rent.

Owning rental real estate is a part-time effort, but if done correctly, it can really accelerate your ability to build income and wealth through the trifecta of leverage, income, and appreciation. Leverage means you're using someone else's (the bank's) money to pay for part of the property in the form of a mortgage. Income is produced from the tenant who pays you rent. Appreciation is what you get over time as the value of the property increases. The challenge here is to make sure you buy the property correctly and the rent pays you more than the cost of the property each month. Let's look at an example of a good rental property and some rules to follow when going down the path of semi-passive income.

Ideally, your property should be in a blue- or grey-collar neighborhood. Prices for this type of home vary across the country, so I'll use an example in Denver where property values and rents are high. If you follow the basic concept here, it should work for where you live.

Generally, single-family homes rent well and have two to four bedrooms for a family. The reason I like blue- and grey-collar areas is most of the time your tenants are hardworking people for whom homeownership is just out of reach, but they have stable jobs and enough income to pay a decent amount in rent.

Come to think of it, those renters should be reading this book! I digress....

Generally, blue- and grey-collar families will take decent care of the home and have sustainable resources to pay rent. In Denver, this type of home costs about $300,000 to $400,000. The rent on these properties is between $2,500 and $3,200 per month at the present time. Your monthly rents should be no more than .80 to 1 percent of the home value per month.

Let's look at a real-life example based on a $300,000 home. In this case, the monthly rent is $2,500, which is a little less than 1 percent of the home value. If you're looking at a $300,000 property and your rent is around 1 percent of the home price, then you need to put 20 percent down on the property to buy it and make the numbers work. At today's low mortgage rates, that property will cost $1,500 per month and maintenance will be 10 percent of rent. Your net rental income each month would be $950, subtracting maintenance, mortgage, and insurance costs. Since you put $60,000 down on the property, it's paying you $950 month, which is a return on investment of 19 percent per year in the form of income. That's tough to beat, isn't it?

In my experience, the best rule to live by in rental property investing is to ensure the property you buy is sound mechanically, it's in a blue- or grey-collar neighborhood, and you are getting at least a 10 percent return in annual cash flow on the cash you put down on the property. Simply put, in this case, if you put $60,000 down, you need to clear $500 per month in cash flow after expenses.

Finally, you need to build a reserve for each property of six months' worth of expenses, so don't plan on using the cash for a while until your reserve is built up.

As with any investment or income strategy, rental real estate is not without its shortcomings. Most people who own rentals will swear they are the best investment they've ever made. You might want to be careful when you hear this since the mechanics of this style of investment are often misrepresented and the rewards are exaggerated. If you don't follow the rules we discussed earlier and buy the properties using the 1 percent and 10 percent rules, you will surely find yourself upside down and backward. Real estate, like all markets, is a market. Prices go up or down based on demand and supply, so it's not a perfect mousetrap—nothing is.

And don't be afraid to hire a management company to take over the maintenance and rent collection for the home. If you're not handy and don't want to deal with people, that is the way to go. You should not pay more than 10 percent of total rents to a management company. If you follow those basic rules, the returns are unmatched unless you own your own business.

ACTIVE INCOME

At the bottom of our income triangle is the active income model. This is, by far, the most lucrative and most challenging income strategy. Active income strategies can be started with very little money. Ideally, you're looking for a way to generate income that requires your effort instead of your money. I'm not talking about going out and getting a J-O-B. I'm talking about the kinds of businesses that can be started as a side hustle and blossom into a recurring-revenue machine.

According to Investopedia, the recurring-income model is defined as the portion of a company's revenue expected to continue into the future. Unlike the one-time sale of a product, these revenues are predictable, stable, and can be counted on to occur at regular intervals going forward with a relatively high degree of certainty. In other words, any business or side hustle you start should not be an "eat what you kill" model. Your revenue should come in whether or not you made a sale or finished a project, and whether or not you showed up to the office on a given day. Over my nineteen-year career as a financial services provider (recurring-revenue model), I've had a front row seat to the very best active income business models with recurring revenue.

Since there are many models, I've spent some time researching and compiling the best models I've seen, which I will list below. Most of them require very little cash to start up, but they do require a regular dose of elbow grease. I'll also give you a short description of each model to pique your interest. For the most part, these businesses can sell easily because any potential buyer would be looking for ongoing revenue to justify their investment. These types of businesses could eventually lead to a work-optional lifestyle through the sale of the business or stepping back to hire someone who can run it well.

Subscription for Services: This model is one of the best I've seen for those who have a very specific skillset to offer the general public. Instead of billing the user when the work or project is done, you charge a monthly subscription for your service. Some good examples I've seen are tax preparation and planning, financial planning, business consulting and coaching, web design, and marketing. Instead of charging by the hour or by the project, a subscription model ties the client to the service as an ongoing engagement, and in my view, tends to produce better outcomes as long as your end user knows what they are getting for that monthly charge. Your revenue is predictable, and generally, the client is happier to pay a low monthly cost. I've seen examples of this model increase my own business as well as countless others. There is no one-time-purchase commission, and the client feels comfortable engaging at any time with no end to the relationship.

Recurring Commission Sales: One of my close friends started selling internet connections to small businesses in his late twenties. With each sale, he received a small portion of the monthly bill as an ongoing commission. At the time, he was working for a local telecom provider and slowly built up his clientele and his recurring revenue. After a few short years, he started brokering the different telecom providers and hired others to sell for him. Other clients of mine have used this model by selling insurance and collecting a commission on each premium, whether it's health insurance, property and casualty insurance, or general lines of commercial insurance. Recurring commission sales can be a fantastic way to earn income while you're sleeping. The one danger in this model is you have to watch out for industry disruption or commoditization of the thing you're selling. For instance, many go online now to purchase insurance or telecom, so unless you're part of the online marketplace, it can be very difficult for you to sell.

Property Management: Are you handy around the house? Perhaps you're already in construction or one of the trades? I really like this business for people who know their way around when it comes to working on a house. You can start this business for virtually nothing but a set of tools and a website. The beauty in this business is you can charge a percentage of rent to take care of someone's properties. Let's say they rent their home for $1,500 a month and you charge 10 percent of rent to manage their property. That's $150 in recurring income each month, whether or not something goes wrong with the house. If you do a great job, you'll undoubtedly get referred around to multiple clients and build a really cool business. Aside from the fact that this business is fairly hands-on, it is a great model and can grow quickly.

Network Marketing: This type of business opportunity is very popular with people looking for part-time, flexible businesses. Network marketing programs feature a low upfront cost, usually only a few hundred dollars for the purchase of products or samples. You initially capitalize on the opportunity by promoting the product line directly to friends, family, and other personal contacts. Most network marketing programs also ask participants to recruit other sales representatives. The recruits constitute a rep's "downline," and their sales generate income for those above them in the program. I can say from personal experience that this type of business has made many people I know very good incomes for part-time work. One word of advice here is to make sure you believe in what the company offers and you are committed to success despite how many nos you hear along the way.

Newsletter Service: A good friend of mine happens to have an incredible, even absurd knowledge of the budding cannabis industry (no pun intended) in the United States and how to invest in it. He once provided me a copy of what he was sending along to family and friends who were interested in the topic. His work was incredible, and his advice in the newsletter was actionable. I felt he had a good opportunity to expand this concept. I suggested he start charging for a subscription to his newsletter or at least post his vast knowledge online and begin asking for a small monthly payment or an email address so he could build a subscription base either through paying customers, ad revenue, or affiliate marketing (which I'll explain next). Newsletters are a great way to build an audience and an income model based on specific expertise you have. Once you build a dedicated fanbase that really values your intellect and your knowledge, it becomes a business you can do from anywhere and pays over and over again once your audience has bought in.

Affiliate Marketing and Blogging: I have less personal experience with this type of business, but based on my research, it is a very good opportunity to add some extra income if you have skills in the online marketplace. Affiliate marketing is a marketing arrangement in which an online retailer pays commission to an external website for traffic or sales generated from its referrals. In other words, you can post an ad on your newsletter or blog for something related to the specific area of your expertise and earn a commission based on any sales resulting from that ad. Even the famed Mr. Money Mustache blog (a great blog about financial independence) has ads for credit cards that offer the best deals and reward points programs.

Let's say your website is a subscription service for weight loss where you blog about success stories and sell your services to potential members. Wouldn't it be a symbiotic pleasure to promote another vendor who sells organic meal plans so your customers can stick to your method? Let's say each referral from your website to the meal plan company makes you a $15 commission. Let's say 100 of your subscribers click through the ad and buy a subscription. The quick math says that's $1,500 in your pocket for very little effort!

STEPPING OVER DOLLARS TO GET TO PENNIES

Within the context of these business methods, I want to illustrate a critical misstep you could make as you're identifying which active income model works best for you. Don't step over dollars to get to pennies. If you've ever heard that phrase before, it means don't be afraid to spend money to enhance return on your time and capital. I'm going to illustrate this concept a couple of different ways with real-life examples.

Imagine you've set up a couple of rental properties that are running smoothly, but you find yourself constantly going over to make repairs and collect rent. You could hire a property management service, but you don't want to part with the 10 percent of your rent it would cost you. Over time, you've spent about six or seven hours per month managing the rental business you built. For a couple of hundred dollars per month, you would get your six or seven hours back and be able to focus on other properties, explore another income venture, or just spend time with your family. All of those things would lead to much larger rewards than a couple of hundred dollars per month. The point here is to be conscious of where your time is spent and how much that costs in not only time, but the value you lose by spending that time.

Another example—let's say you're trying to put your income portfolio together for the passive-income approach, but you've spent hours poring over the available investment options and you still aren't sure which ones to choose. Instead of hiring a professional for $500 to $1,000, you end up buying a few less-than-desirable investments that can't sustain your income. The loss here is compounded because you spent time and lost money in the process. Hiring a professional to do this for you would save you time and leverage someone's years of experience and education in positioning your investments for the long term.

Finally, let's say you've started your active-income business and things are going well, but you know there's another level you could reach if you hire a coach or a web design service to enhance your reach and talent. The coach costs $2,500, and you just don't want to spend that kind of money, so you spend hours and hours researching best practices and even more hours designing your website with no previous programming experience. You could spend the money and get back all your time, leverage someone else's resources, and make ten times your investment back in profits. This is a critical mistake I have seen played out over and over again. Don't be the person who steps over dollars to get to pennies! After all, if you've built your super reserve and are generating income, this shouldn't be a concern.

PUTTING IT ALL TOGETHER

The income triangle is the method behind your work-optional life. If you've followed the plan up to this point, then it's time to make the jump. Which areas of the triangle might work for you? Make your decision and follow that yellow brick road. All of these three paths (passive, semi-passive, or active) can lead you to financial independence and a work-optional life. Your job is to expand your mind and choose a path right now. You can choose one and add another as time goes on, but you must choose. So, what will it be?

CHALLENGE 9

Choose an area of the triangle to focus on and ask yourself these questions:

If you choose an active income model, which of the six branches of active income fit your personality and skills?

If you choose passive income, whom will you hire to help you choose which investments to use? Are you going to do this yourself?

If you like the semi-passive portion of the triangle, what's your budget for the rental property, and how much money will you put down?

Now, let's make a declaration! I (insert name) ____________ will focus my energy and financial resources on creating a work-optional lifestyle with $________ coming in every month from ____________ (passive, active or semi active income) by (date) ________.

Now you have built your super reserve and set a goal for the amount of income you will need and identified one of the income strategies to use to achieve your goal. What specifically are you going to do first to generate that income? If it's passive income, are you going to use the rule of 250 and hire a financial planner, or set up a brokerage account? If it's active income, be specific about the business you are going to start and the first step you need to take. If it's semi-active income, determine the amount you will need to save toward a down payment on your first property. Take action immediately, and continue making steps forward. Remember, you're now in a great financial position with your super reserve to start making these choices. Revisit this declaration often to measure your progress.

full
part
time

Chapter 10

CHANGE

"Change is the law of life. And those who look only to the past or present are certain to miss the future."

— John F. Kennedy

THE STRUGGLE IS REAL

You've now learned about the path to living a work-optional life and have the strategies to get you there. Once you've implemented the strategies and started living a new way, change will inevitably happen. You will face stumbles, bumbles, and fumbles along the way. You may have a setback in achieving your super reserve, one of your businesses might fall on hard times, or an investment in real estate may be more than you bargained for. You will have moments that feel painful along your journey to a work-optional lifestyle. With that in mind, let me lay out some strategies you can use to cope with change and stay on your path to a better life. These tools will give you the extra boost you'll need to get through hard times, and if implemented correctly, they may even make the journey better than you imagined. We're all prone to making bad decisions, and we're certainly vulnerable to the bad decisions others make, so it's important to keep our wits about us and stay above the fray.

Let's get started with some tools you can use.

YOU CAN'T DO WELL IF YOU DON'T FEEL WELL

Staying physically and mentally healthy is critical to achieving a work-optional lifestyle. You can't do well if you don't feel well. Regular exercise produces endorphins in the body. Endorphins originate in the brain's hypothalamus and pituitary gland and are structurally similar to the drug morphine. So, essentially, your body produces natural painkillers when you get regular exercise, and these chemicals ultimately reduce discomfort. Being financially successful and sticking to a new plan can certainly cause mental and physical discomfort. Why wouldn't you want as many of these self-produced endorphins as you can get so they can help bring about positive feelings and general well-being? Here's the best part about these drugs—they're free!

Go on a run before you tackle your next monthly budget. Get a bike ride in before you sit down to write your monthly newsletter. Start a routine of exercising at least two to three days per week. This can be as simple as a walk around the block or a spin on your stationary bike. The key is to schedule the time on the calendar and stick to it for at least sixty days so you can build the habit of being physically active and healthy.

Earlier, we talked about money karma where things just start going right financially because you have achieved discipline with your money. In my opinion, the same holds true with physical fitness. You begin to lose weight, and then your cholesterol improves. You start exercising at a gym and meet the right person. Perhaps you join a cycling club, and the contacts you make through it end up being good for business. The list goes on, and in my experience, a universal principle is at work here. Doing the right thing attracts more right things.

It's also helpful to look at the opposite side of feeling well and exercising regularly. Have you ever had that feeling of abdominal discomfort after a fast-food lunch? Have you ever drank too much and felt crappy the next day? I know I've had my fair share of those days. After those experiences, I felt bad about myself, my body felt sluggish, and my brain felt clouded. I knew that was not the way I wanted to travel through life, so I made the choice to cut out fast food and too much alcohol.

Perhaps you run out of breath after climbing the stairs? Without an exercise routine, we lack energy and are sapped of our ability to perform at our highest level. Volumes have been written on exercise and nutrition—enough to get lost in for years. But the hard truth is it's simply a choice, and we have to bargain with ourselves. We choose to be lazy, eat crappy food, and drink crappy drinks. We also choose to eat good, healthy food and walk around the block a few times a week.

Either way, fit or fat, we are far more likely to push through a financial struggle if we feel good and exercise regularly. We are far less likely to push through a financial obstacle if we feel lethargic and melancholy.

So, schedule exercise two or three times a week, and let me know how you feel about yourself and your finances after two months. Odds are, those endorphins will be kicking in, and you will feel good about where you are and where you're headed!

GET UP EARLY

Imagine if you had 260 hours more each year to work on your mental, physical, and financial health? Do you think you would make some progress? That's the amount of time you can add into your life by simply getting up an hour earlier each weekday. After coaching thousands of clients, I always hear the excuse, "I don't have time to budget," or "I don't have time to research my next business idea." I always contrast that response with my most successful clients who always seem to get things done and become more financially successful than the rest. Believe it or not, I ask many of them what time they get up in the morning. Without question, those who have more wealth get up early. Those who are less disciplined and seem to struggle usually get up later in the morning.

The processes you've learned thus far take time to implement and mental fortitude to keep going. My favorite book on this subject is Hal Elrod's *The Miracle Morning*. Before I read it, I was personally struggling with finding time to exercise and get organized for my day. I always felt rushed, and by the time I got to the office, I was consumed by the tyranny of the urgent. Does that sound familiar? Then I read Elrod's book. Nowadays, I get up between 5:00 and 5:30 a.m. I work out for an hour, then meditate and journal for another twenty minutes. I feel like a million bucks! I've even been throwing around the idea of 4:30 a.m. since 5:00 worked so well—call me crazy. Since I've implemented the tactics in Hal's book, I'm happier, in better shape, and my productivity has gone through the roof. If you're focused on achieving a work-optional lifestyle, getting up early will give you the time you need to focus on your plan. If you can get at least one more hour each day, your chances of success dramatically improve.

We have twenty-four hours in a day, and most of us need seven hours of sleep. That leaves seventeen hours to accomplish our goals. We work eight to ten hours a day during the week, so let's say we work ten hours. That leaves seven hours a day, and let's figure three hours of eating, socializing, and commuting. We're left with four hours to work on this plan. What could you accomplish with four hours a day? That's 1,040 hours a year to budget, plan your business, work on your philosophy, pay off your debts, and generate income, and I haven't even accounted for weekends. Go ahead and set that alarm a few minutes earlier each day and see what you can accomplish. If you're able to push just one hour a day by waking up earlier during the work week, that's 260 hours in the bank for this plan. The early bird truly gets the worm, and it's a great way to focus on yourself, your needs, and the journey to your work-optional life.

HAVE A PHILOSOPHY

While you're up in the morning a little earlier, perhaps you can spend a few minutes on your philosophy of life. In his book *Win Forever*, Pete Carroll talks about making sure you have a philosophy to live by. Carroll is the head coach of the Super Bowl winning Seattle Seahawks. He developed his philosophy over many years while coaching and learning about what it takes to win. To make a long story short, Carroll found that competition is the key to making people perform at their best. He determined that if you are fighting for your job every day, you're more likely to excel at it.

Carroll's philosophy of life is "Win Forever." That means winning is a way of life for him and his personal mantra. He breaks down his philosophy into four basic parts, which all start with a foundation and a belief system to live by. As an example, a belief system might be to always follow the golden rule, always tell the truth, or always control your emotions.

Then, above the belief system, is the critical theme to live by. In Carroll's case, it's competition—everything is a competition, so you do your very best at every moment.

Then the philosophy moves upward into the environment that competition and the belief system create. The environment Carroll's philosophy creates for him and his players is that practice is everything. So, within the sport of football, Carroll believes if you perform during practice by being more competitive than anyone else, you can have the confidence at game time to put forth a winning effort. From there, the belief system, the environment, and the critical theme creates a winning performance on the field. My personal life philosophy is "Be Better," which means that each day I must strive to improve upon who I was yesterday. The environment I create for myself is one in which I can keep getting better at the mental, physical, and spiritual aspects of my life each day. If I have a lousy day and know I didn't improve on who I was yesterday, it really gets to me. It means I'm not executing my philosophy of being better. Having a personal life philosophy is an accountability system for you and only you. Ultimately, you are your worst critic, and if you have a philosophy to live by, the critic in you has a basis on which to judge. If there is no basis and no judge, there is no direction and no success.

Finally, if you don't have a way of life and a philosophy to live by, then the accumulation of money and freedom will have less value for you. Your philosophy of life might be as simple as "Family first," "Work hard to play hard," or "Give glory to God"—you get the drift. Develop a mantra and a philosophy no matter how simple. This is the overarching principle for living your life each day. This is true north on the compass of your life. A lot can be found in Greek philosophy and by spiritual guides on this subject. I truly believe it will help you. At the very least, search "how to develop a personal philosophy," and you'll find volumes to help you home in on one that fits you and your lifestyle.

IT'S NEVER TOO LATE

Clichéd as it may sound, it's never too late to start your plan. If you're older, there is still a ton of hope for you. Ray Kroc didn't start McDonald's until he was fifty-two. Of course, Kroc had a philosophy for the company: "Quality, Service, Cleanliness, and Value." That philosophy created a worldwide, multi-billion-dollar fast food empire. The fast-food restaurant he started late in life created a few bucks of active income for Kroc and his family for many generations to come. Colonel Sanders, otherwise known as Harland Sanders, was broke and living in his car at age sixty-two when he started the first Kentucky Fried Chicken restaurant. Julia Child didn't publish her first cookbook until age thirty-nine and debuted in her first cooking show when she was fifty-one. Laura Ingalls Wilder, the author of the *Little House on the Prairie* series, didn't have her first book published until she was sixty-five. I could go on, but the point is, these people all found their true north late in life and became successful.

Managing your money the right way can also happen at any stage of life if you have a reason to make it happen and a practical money plan and philosophy to guide you along the way. As we get older, our excuses seem to pile up like we're collecting them to someday pass on to our kids. It's not too late; it's never too late to live your work-optional life. Just because there's less distance in the windshield than in the rearview mirror doesn't mean you can't take a right turn and change the destination of your life.

The principles you've just learned are key to maximizing your bandwidth for success. The environment you create around yourself breeds success and allows room to follow this plan to enhance your life. If you could master just one of these areas, which one would it be? Are you going to get up earlier and create more time to focus on your money? If you do, I've just given you a way to free up at least 260 hours to work on this plan. Are you going to build a philosophy that drives every decision you make in the same direction so that you can act with purpose? Are you going to start a workout routine and walk around the block every morning to clear your head and focus on the plan? Have you decided it's not too late to get going on this plan and act right now to make a difference for yourself and your family? Choose something from this chapter to implement, dog-ear this chapter, and come back to it once you've mastered one of these principles. Then come back and master another one. I promise, life will be better and this plan will make room for you.

(See the Challenge on the next page)

CHALLENGE 10

Think about the challenges you have today and the challenges you are going to face in the future. Would it benefit you to feel a little better physically? Perhaps you need another hour in your day. Maybe your spirit could use a little conditioning, and you could build a better philosophy for your life. What is one small change in routine or philosophy you can make today that will help you better cope with the struggles headed your way? I'm going to list out a few options, and I'd encourage you to circle one and focus on it for one year. Then report back to yourself to see if your life has changed for the better.

- I will get up earlier each day to work on myself (define the time).
- I will build my life philosophy (write it down and look at it every day).
- I will work out at least (define how many days a week).
- I will eat better to be at my target weight of (define your target weight).

These activities will help you cope with struggle and help you become a more rounded and resilient person. You should consider writing these items down in a separate location to look at every single day when you get up. Revisit this list each year in combination with your work-optional income goals. Update the list as your life unfolds and I promise you won't be disappointed with the results.

full
part
time

A Final Note

LEAVE A LEGACY

"So live your life that the fear of death can never enter your heart. Trouble no one about their religion; respect others in their view, and demand that they respect yours. Love your life, perfect your life, beautify all things in your life. Seek to make your life long and its purpose in the service of your people."

— Chief Tecumseh

We've been through a lot together thus far. The final phase of your work-optional life is upon us. The plan you're making should be beautiful and in the service of your people. Chief Tecumseh (1768-1813) was a Native American Shawnee warrior celebrated as one of the most influential Native American leaders in history. He was especially talented at oration and bringing multiple tribes together to fight American expansion into the Midwest during the late 1700s and early 1800s. He was even bestowed with the honor of becoming a brigadier general for the British shortly before the War of 1812. I digress, but his words above form one of the most beautiful passages I have ever read. It was featured in the 2012 movie *Act of Valor* depicting our modern-day warrior Navy Seals in a worldwide manhunt.

What's beautiful about this quote is it sums up what life should be about: serving your people and making your life beautiful. Your people can mean your family, your kids, other families, and those less fortunate. Making it beautiful can mean leaving a legacy of wealth intentionally designed to help others, improving everything you touch, or raising a family with beauty and grace. This passage sums up the elegance of life and what we're all hopefully after, which is to make a difference and create beauty each day. Life is not easy; it can be tragic and there is a lot of suffering, but remembering this passage can lead you to examine what you are to do each day despite all the misgivings of being alive. You can use it as a guidepost to see where you are headed each day. I have a copy of the full passage in my garage so I can see it daily when I pull in and out to do my duty and serve my people. To make your life beautiful is a mission that never ends—to serve one another is also a mission that never ends. There is no peak to the journey and no downhill slide if you keep your vision.

In the spirit of making your life beautiful, you must have a final plan for when you go over the great divide. Write down a special way to divide the assets you worked so hard to build. Set up a will and appoint someone to look after your medical and financial needs if you are unable to take care of yourself. The best way to do this is to hire an attorney who has done work for a friend or colleague. It's worth the investment to make sure your wishes are carried out exactly how you want them. When it's all buttoned up at the end, your family will appreciate you even more.

You will also want to write a letter to those you love telling them how much you love them. I call this the family love letter. When I wrote mine to my children, I could barely get through the tears as I was writing about what I saw in them and how much I appreciated having them in my life. I also told them what I thought was unique about each of them and closed the letter by letting them know I will always be with them. This exercise added a beautiful light to designing my final plan and motivated me to make it easy for them if something ever happens to me. I also left some money to charities and causes I believe in so that my legacy can live on in the causes that are dear to my heart.

My challenge to you is never to peak in your life journey, your financial journey, and your service to others. The FIRE (financial independence retire early) movement that has gained so much notoriety as of late is flawed because it assumes there is a magical end to your struggle. It asks you to deprive yourself of many things to live out a selfish journey of frugality and lack so you can retire early. Who cares? How about living your financial life on purpose and giving yourself choices? How about not following the masses and creating an unstoppable life that continues to compound on itself and allows you to follow your creative desires and make decisions on your terms?

If you're on that journey, you will never peak. You will find yourself going from one beautiful challenge to another with complete financial confidence so you can follow where your soul leads.

I wish you much success, happiness, and prosperity on that journey!

ABOUT THE AUTHOR

Jeremy Davis is a proud father of two, a personal wealth advisor since 2002, and an avid mountain biker and skier. He has been on a mission since his early twenties to help others become financially successful.

Jeremy is a Certified Financial Planner Professional and Chartered Financial Consultant, and he holds the Certified Retirement Plans Specialist and Accredited Portfolio Management Advisor credentials. He's worked with more than 1,000 families to help them achieve their goals. In the process, he has noticed common misconceptions and mistakes made by many of them.

Each time Jeremy sat down with a client to discuss their future, he used the term "work-optional lifestyle" to describe retirement. Without hesitation, almost all of his clients gravitated to this concept as a way of making sense of their own retirement beliefs. After some encouragement from many of those clients, Jeremy decided to write this book as an instruction manual so everyone can achieve the work-optional lifestyle he has helped so many of his clients accomplish. He set out to demystify the process of retirement planning and ended up creating a very successful financial planning practice along the way. If you are interested in creating a work-optional lifestyle, *Living Your Work-Optional Lifestyle* is your toolkit for success.

NOTES

NOTES